Contents

Complaints Panels
in Social Care

iams

Russell House Publishing

First published in 2010 by:
Russell House Publishing Ltd.
4 St. George's House
Uplyme Road
Lyme Regis
Dorset DT7 3LS
Tel: 01297-443948
Fax: 01297-442722
e-mail: help@russellhouse.co.uk
www.russellhouse.co.uk

© Catherine Williams and Katy Ferris

The moral right of Catherine Williams and Katy Ferris to be identified as the authors of this work has been asserted by them in accordance with The Copyright, Designs and Patents Act 1988.

British Library Cataloguing-in-publication Data:
A catalogue record for this book is available from the British Library.

ISBN: 978-1-905541-65-2

Typeset by TW Typesetting, Plymouth, Devon

Printed and bound in Great Britain by
CPI Antony Rowe, Chippenham and Eastbourne

About Russell House Publishing

RHP is a group of social work, probation, education and youth and community work practitioners and academics working in collaboration with a professional publishing team.

Our aim is to work closely with the field to produce innovative and valuable materials to help managers, trainers, practitioners and students.

We are keen to receive feedback on publications and new ideas for future projects.

For details of our other publications please visit our website or ask us for a catalogue. Contact details are on this page.

Preface

This book is a guide to the process and experience of complaints panels in social care, in work both with adults and with children and young people. Whilst underpinned by the legal requirements for setting up a panel, it:

- offers further information on how panels should be run
- suggests how to avoid potential problems
- gives advice on achieving 'best practice'.

The book aims to enhance the development of panels.

The book covers all aspects of the panel procedure, from the setting up of a panel through to the panel recommendations being referred to the director for his decision. The chapters include a summary of key issues, which will be of assistance in overcoming problems which may be encountered in the panel process.

During the empirical research which formed the basis of this book, it became evident that many local authority complaints managers were not aware of how other authorities were conducting panels and that, beyond the legislation and Department of Health guidance, there was no up-to-date guide to assist them in reviewing their procedure. This book offers an opportunity for all readers to learn from the experiences of other local authorities. It identifies potential pitfalls and demonstrates good practice in complaints handling.

The intended readership is primarily:

- those people who are responsible for the panel procedure within a local authority
- those staff who may be called to the panel
- members of panels
- those studying the practice of social care.

Complaints managers, who have the day-to-day responsibility for handling complaints, will find the sections on chairing the panel especially helpful in any training or guidance they may want to provide to their independent people.

Those complaints managers who are charged with the responsibility of overhauling their complaints procedure will also find it of particular use as a benchmark guide.

It will help **directors of social care** in their responses to panel recommendations, and in aiding them to know whether their panel procedure is the best it can be.

Due to an increasing involvement of advocates and the need for legal advice in the complaints process, the book will assist people in understanding what **advocates and their clients** can, and should, expect from the experience.

For anyone new to social care complaints, whether in the running of the procedure or as an independent panel member, this book offers an introduction to the requirements and procedure of panels.

Those who are appointed as independent people, that is **independent persons, investigators and panel members**, will find the book very helpful as it guides them through the panel process. The book carefully explains their roles and uses real case study examples from which to learn. Those in the role of **panel chair** will find it particularly useful.

Finally, the book is also aimed at **those studying social care**, either as a teacher or a student. In our modern society, users of services are increasingly encouraged to come forward with their complaints, both as a means of remedying individual deficiencies and, on the larger front, as a means to improve services more generally. It is therefore of importance to all involved in studying the system to have a full understanding of the key issues and processes.

Note: the law applies to England and Wales in exactly the same way. There are very similar systems in place in Scotland and Northern Ireland and this book should also be relevant in those areas.

Acknowledgements

We would like to thank all our independent person colleagues and the complaints managers we have worked with for providing us with help, support and valuable guidance and information, all of which has assisted greatly in the writing of this book. Special mention must be made of Dick, Ian and Rod, who have not only been excellent colleagues but have also helped by supplying some of the case examples. Further we would like to express appreciation to the local authorities and to the individuals who work in the social care complaints profession who contributed so much to the empirical research by giving up their time and sharing their invaluable experiences.

The authors would like to thank Geoffrey Mann for the opportunity to publish this work and his enthusiasm for the project. Lastly, we would like to say a special thank you to John Charles and Gaynor Goodwin for their continued support and input to our work, for which we are both very grateful.

About the Authors

Catherine Williams was appointed as an independent investigator of complaints and independent chair of panels at the inception of the *Children Act 1989*, in 1991, and has been involved in complaints ever since. She is an honorary reader in law at the University of Sheffield. Catherine has written several articles on the subject of complaints and, with Helen Jordan, wrote an early study on the operation of the complaints procedure in six different local authority areas.

In 2006 **Katy Ferris** completed an empirical PhD of Social Services Complaints Procedures in England and Wales. She is a senior lecturer in law at Sheffield Hallam University and has experience of work as an independent panel member and chair.

Introduction

The empirical research that underpins this book covered 47 out of 150 local authorities in detail and involved five years of study. At least three authorities were included in every single region in England and Wales in the research, which also had input from the local government ombudsmen offices, and a representative from the Children's Commissioner for Wales. Interviews were also conducted with many chairs of panels, including both those who work independently and people who work for an agency.

Every local authority must have a complaints procedure in place in order for people in receipt of social care to have an avenue of complaint and to comply with the *Health and Social Care Act* 2003. The legal requirements of Social Care Complaints panels have been changed in the last few years, but local authorities still retain quite considerable discretion in the way that they form and run panels. This book therefore aims to provide guidance and assistance, and to disseminate good practice to professionals at all levels involved in running and taking part in the procedure.

The culmination of the complaints procedure is a panel hearing, when three people consider the complaint based upon the investigation. Panels have wide powers. These powers include upholding or rejecting decisions made by the local authority, as well as asking the local authority to reconsider a decision in respect of the complainant. Panels can also make financial recommendations.

The book breaks down the panel process into the following key elements:

Chapter 1: Introduction to the complaints procedure and panels

We explain the background to the complaints procedure, with reference to the empirical research and recent government changes.

Chapter 2: The constitution of the panel

This chapter considers the panel members in detail. The appointment of panel members can often cause problems when local authorities are convening the panel. Consideration is given to the different options the local authority has, the independence of members and any training they should have.

Chapter 3: Arrangements for the panel hearing

This chapter looks at the actions which need to be taken to help ensure that the panel is compliant with legislation, whilst helping to ensure that those attending the panel are comfortable with the arrangements. It focuses on the information which needs to be provided to the parties attending, as well as giving consideration to the venues which might be considered suitable for the panel hearing.

Chapter 4: The panel hearing

This chapter covers the panel hearing process on the day. It considers in detail the role of those attending and the procedure, advising as to best practice for running the hearing. It considers the pre-panel meeting, the actual hearing and how best to keep a record of the panel.

Chapter 5: Recommendations of the panel

This chapter covers what happens in order for the panel to come to their conclusions; the types of recommendations, which may be made; time limits for making the recommendations; who is involved at the recommendation stage; and confidentiality. In addition we tackle the situation where a panel are not in agreement.

Chapter 6: Procedure after the panel

The final focus is on procedures after the panel has concluded its deliberations. The issues that are considered are: the time taken to respond to the complainant informing them of the outcome; to whom the recommendations are sent in order for the local authority to consider its final response; methods of communication between the chair and director after the panel; and whether the recommendations are followed and if this is done successfully.

All six of the chapters include real case studies, providing examples and learning points for the reader.

When using the first person singular, other than in the real cases and examples where the actual gender of the people involved is used, for ease of writing we have followed an accepted convention of referring to people in the masculine gender. There is, however, one exception to this. As we are both female chairs of panels, we refer throughout to the chair in the feminine gender.

We refer to people by the same title throughout the book. Therefore, the person who is responsible for the complaints process is always called the complaints manager and his workplace the complaints unit. The person representing the department at panel is called the adjudicating officer and the investigator is called the investigating officer. The person to whom the panel findings and recommendations are sent is called the director.

Copying Permissions and Multiple Copy Discounts

Using the material from this book within your organisation

RHP encourages all organisations who want to copy **small amounts** of copyright material from this and other books for one-off use (on a significant number of occasions) to obtain a license from the Copyright Licensing Agency (see page ii), whose goal is to make reasonable copying simple and fair.

Most local authorities and universities already have CLA licences. Please be sure to make sure you know the terms of the licence before making any copies from this book. Please understand that in CLA licences:

- 'Small amounts' of copying means no more than a single chapter or 5% of the book.

- Systematic copying of single chapters in turn is not permitted.

- Storage of material for regular use is not permitted.

- Copying of anything beyond 'small amounts' is not permitted.

Purchasers of this manual who wish to make **larger amounts** of material from this book available to colleagues on a regular basis may **buy multiple copies of the manual at a discount . . .** RHP can offer significant discounts to anyone wishing to buy four or more copies of this manual at any one time. Please contact help@russellhouse.co.uk for further details, including our terms and conditions.

Chapter 1

Introduction to the Complaints Procedure and Panels

Prior to 1991, a service user of social services, as it was then called,[1] did not have recourse to any statutorily based complaints procedure should they have cause for complaint. Some local authorities did have their own individual systems but they were set up on a purely ad hoc basis and there was no consistency around the country. However, the *NHS and Community Care Act 1990*,[2] in relation to adults, and the *Children Act 1989*[3] introduced a requirement whereby local authorities became statutorily bound to establish a complaints procedure in their social services, now social care, departments. The provisions came into force in October 1991. The government at the time had claimed that the complaints procedures:

> *will be an essential safeguard for users and will also act as an important monitoring and management instrument for social services authorities and service providers alike.*[4]

The importance of having such a complaints procedure for children was particularly exposed by events at two children's homes, which arose prior to the implementation date of October 1991. Children had been complaining about abuse taking place at these homes, yet nothing had been done about it. The inquiry report from *Pindown* in Staffordshire was published in 1991[5] and then, in 1993, following the conviction of Frank Beck for sexual abuse of children within Leicestershire children's homes, two further reports were published.[6] The widespread concern about what had been happening in the homes was at least partly addressed by the statutory measures contained in the *Children Act*. After the publication of the first of these reports (*Pindown*) the Department of Health issued a circular[7] which detailed steps which should be taken in the light of the report findings. It further emphasised that:

> *The Secretary of State also considers that the Staffordshire Report demonstrates the need for complaints procedures which are clearly accessible to and understood by all children in residential care and involve an independent element.*[8]

The *Children Act* and the *NHS and Community Care Act* both required the local authority to have an established complaints procedure, which provides an accessible and effective means of representation for adults and children alike. The aim of the procedure is to allow any individual in receipt of social care to have his problems heard and at the same time to provide an important learning opportunity for the relevant service. The adult and child procedures, which were almost identical in content, continued in tandem until 2009, when, on 1 April, new regulations on the joint social care and health complaints procedure came into force.[9] In light of the changes to the new adult regulations, hereafter all reference to the complaints procedure will be to the children's procedure.

The basic procedure for complaints in social care

There are three stages to the complaints procedure, with timescales for resolution of the complaint at each stage:

- **Stage 1: Local resolution (10–20 working days)**
  At Stage 1 complaints are dealt with by the manager at the point closest to the service. The vast majority of complaints are resolved at this stage.

- **Stage 2: Investigation (25–65 working days)**
  Where a complaint has not been resolved at Stage 1, or is too complex to allow for local resolution, the complaint proceeds to Stage 2. At this stage an investigator is appointed, who must either be an internal investigator, but someone independent of the service complained about, or an external independent investigator. In addition, an independent person must also be appointed. This person is appointed to ensure that the investigation is properly carried out. Of those complaints which are investigated at Stage 2, again the vast majority are resolved at this stage.

- **Stage 3: Complaints review panel (30 working days)**
  Where it has still not been possible to resolve the complaint after an investigation, because the complainant is not satisfied with either the investigation, or the adjudication stemming from the investigation, the complainant can request that the complaint proceeds to a panel for further consideration. The panel must consist of three independent people, who make findings and recommendations for the director, who then makes a decision on the complaint and any action to be taken. It is this stage that is the subject of this book.

Stage 3 completes the statutory complaints procedure. Should the complainant still be dissatisfied, they can then proceed to ask the Local Government Ombudsman to look into the case.

Judicial review and the complaints procedure

Rather than using the complaints procedure, some aggrieved complainants might wish to take their grievance to court. However, judicial review will never be an alternative to the internal mechanisms for complaining. A complainant must normally exhaust all avenues before making an application for judicial review. In *R v. London Borough of Brent, ex parte S*[10] it was confirmed that for a complainant to be allowed to proceed to judicial review before exhausting the complaints procedure it would have to be a case involving exceptional circumstances. In the earlier case of *R v. Secretary of State for the Home Department, ex parte Swati*[11] the Court of Appeal recognised that generally 'exceptional circumstances' defy definition and each case would have to be distinguished and be of particular importance. Further guidance as to when there might be an exception to the rule of having to exhaust internal procedures can be gleaned from the case of *R v. Birmingham City Council, ex parte A*[12] where the Court of Appeal outlined the general position. They said:

Much depends on the nature of the relief sought in the judicial review proceedings, the urgency of the matter and, of course, the facts of the case as compared with what is available in the alternative remedy to meet the justice of the case.

The Court of Appeal compared the situation in the *Birmingham* case with that in *R v. London Borough of Sutton, ex parte Tucker.*[13] In the *Tucker* case the applicant for judicial review was the mother of a young woman with profound disabilities who was placed for assessment in an NHS establishment in November 1993. The assessment was completed in April 1994 and within three months all relevant parties agreed that the young woman was fit to be discharged. However, two years and three months later the young woman was still in the care of the NHS. The mother applied in judicial review for an order of mandamus to compel the local authority to make suitable provision for her daughter. Judge Hidden considered at the time of granting the order, whether the mother could have used the complaints procedure instead of seeking judicial review. He said that she should not have been expected to, as she was seeking relief which was peremptory in nature, her daughter having suffered a considerable delay. He pointed out that had the mother used the complaints procedure she would have had to do so as a non-legally aided person and would therefore have been forced to argue points of law unaided. This was compounded by the fact that the people listening to such points would also have been non-legally qualified. He therefore stated that this would not be 'convenient, expeditious or effective' and in reality there was no real alternative remedy. This was in direct contrast to the *Birmingham* case, where the relief being sought was merely declaratory, the delay had been months rather than years and the local authority had acknowledged its failure to take action. Therefore, judicial review was not the appropriate remedy, rather it was the complaints procedure.

Quite apart from the usual need to exhaust internal procedures first before proceeding to judicial review, there are also some crucial differences between judicial review and the complaints procedure. Originally there was no stipulated time limit for making a complaint under the complaints procedure, although a new requirement that the complaint must be brought within 12 months was introduced in 2006.[14] This is in contrast to judicial review, where a complainant must initiate proceedings within three months of the disputed decision. Perhaps more crucially, the remedies available under judicial review are limited in a way, which is not the case with the complaints procedure.[15]

Jurisdiction of the procedure

Particularly in light of the split between adults' and children's services, dating from April 2009, the issue as to whether or not a complaint falls within the children's procedure has now become even more crucial than it was prior to this date. The reason for this is due to the different requirements imposed by the two procedures and the differing nature of the process. Whilst the children's procedure requires an independent person to be appointed at Stage 2, there is no such requirement under the adult procedure, even including where the adult is a vulnerable adult. Additionally, while the children's procedure automatically allows the complainant to proceed to panel if dissatisfied at the end of Stage 2, the adult procedure no longer places any requirement on the authority to set up a panel. It will only be if they choose to do so that a panel will take place.

Generally speaking the independent person will not have a major role to play in an investigation, only being appointed in order to ensure that a proper investigation has taken place. However, the importance of the independent person is vital if there is any dispute over the quality or outcome of the investigation. Then it is essential that the independent person, when putting in his separate report, details the flaws, as he sees it, with the investigation and any different findings and/or conclusions that the independent person has reached [see case example 1]. Clearly where this occurs, unless the complainant and the authority both agree either with the investigator or with the independent person, which is unlikely, the dispute between the parties needs to proceed to panel, for a third party to make a final decision.

The other major difference, the lack of an automatic right to proceed to panel will, in general, operate to the disadvantage of the complainant. If a complainant remains dissatisfied after an investigation then that is the end of the road, as far as he is concerned, in relation to the complaints procedure.[16] His next step would have to be to take his case on to the Local Government Ombudsman. However, where an authority is not happy with an investigation it may simply choose to ignore, or water down, the findings and recommendations of the investigating officer. Again, if the complainant is dissatisfied with this his only recourse is to the Local Government Ombudsman.

Despite not having to arrange an adult panel, it may be that the authority might choose to set one up. Under the new procedures, before signing off a complaint the senior manager responsible must be satisfied that all reasonable steps have been taken to resolve the complaint.[17] The occasions when the authority might choose to arrange a panel are likely to occur in one of three situations. First, if the complainant is dissatisfied with the investigation and its outcome, the authority might prefer to set up a panel, rather than face an Ombudsman investigation. Secondly, if there has been a poor investigation, leaving both the authority and the complainant dissatisfied, a panel might provide the best solution. And, finally, if there has been a contentious report from the investigating officer, finding in favour of the complainant, but the authority disagrees with the report, its conclusions and recommendations, and the authority will not agree to implement the recommendations, again the authority might choose to proceed to set up a panel.

The decision as to whether a complaint does fall within the children's procedure is not necessarily clear cut; there are a number of grey areas. To illustrate this point, an example would be a complaint by foster parents who have alleged that the support they have been given in pursuit of their duties has been deficient in some way. The complaint may be worded so that it relates solely to the foster parents' grievances. On the surface this looks like a complaint by an adult service user and should therefore be considered under the adult procedure. However, there are two reasons why it could be argued that such a complaint should be dealt with under the child procedures. First, the complaint is about children's services and in the *Children Act 1989* foster parents are specifically listed as persons entitled to use the complaints procedure.[18] Secondly, if services supplied to foster parents are not adequate, this deficiency will then impact on the care that the foster parents give to the children in their care, resulting in the children getting a sub-standard level of care. In this case the argument would be that the complaint is really one on behalf of foster children and should therefore be considered under the children's procedure.[19]

Key points summary

- The complaints procedure came into force in October 1991.

- The procedures for both adults and children were almost identical until April 2009, when the adult system changed.

- There are three stages to the children's procedure, with timescales for each stage.

- The panel is Stage 3, the final stage.

- If the complainant is still dissatisfied, his next option is to proceed to the Local Government Ombudsman.

- Judicial review is not an alternative mechanism. Normally the complaints procedure must first be exhausted before an application can be made in judicial review.

- The key differences between the children and adult procedures are that under the children procedure an independent person must be appointed for a child complaint and the complainant has the right to go to panel. There is no longer an absolute right to proceed to panel in adult complaints.

- There are grey areas where the jurisdiction of the two procedures overlap.

Practice illustrations and case examples

1. The crucial role an independent person can play is illustrated by the following case example:

   The internal investigating officer put in a report which did not uphold any of the complainant's several complaints. However, the independent person, in his report, criticised the investigating officer for: not including the independent person at some of the interviews with staff; for the delay in the investigation; and for being late for some of the interviews, which meant the interviews were rushed and the issues not properly explored. Subsequently, at panel, the panel explored these criticisms of the investigating officer, who was unable to defend his actions. The panel went on to uphold many of the complaints.

   This example shows how vital it can be to have a person completely independent of the authority to monitor the way an investigation is carried out. Had the complaint been an adult complaint, in light of the fact that none of the complaints were upheld by the investigating officer, it is likely that the authority would have accepted his report.

2. If there has been an inadequate investigation and no complaints have been upheld it will give the complainant little faith in the system if the authority goes along with the investigation. Many service users will continue to have to use the service provided, which is likely to make matters worse for them. The following is an illustration of a very poor investigation and its outcome:

   The complainant attended a day centre. He and some of the staff at the unit were at loggerheads with one another and the complainant alleged that the staff were now treating him unfairly. Amongst his list of complaints he alleged that the manager of the centre had lost her temper with him after he had reported a serious incident involving himself and another service user, and had insisted on him being interviewed by the police at the day centre, when he did not want to be. He also alleged that after this incident he had been treated differently by staff, being constantly called into the office and rebuked for his behaviour, when in fact he had done nothing wrong. The investigating officer did not uphold either of these complaints and the case proceeded to panel. At panel the members of the panel found serious deficiencies in the investigating officer's report. In relation to the allegation that the complainant was not asked whether or not he would agree to being interviewed by the police at the day centre, the panel found that the report never identified whether or not he was actually asked if he would agree to be interviewed. The investigating officer merely found that his fears of being interviewed were unnecessary, as in the event he did not find it to be an unpleasant or upsetting experience. With regard to the allegation that the complainant was constantly being called into the office, the panel found that the investigating officer had listed a series of occasions when the records showed that the complainant had been into the office. However, the vast majority of these occasions occurred before the incident complained of, rather than after. The panel also found other deficiencies in the report. Fortunately for the panel, the adjudicating officer who attended the panel had prepared very thoroughly for the panel. He was able to answer all the panel's queries, backing up his answers with very detailed files which he brought with him. As a result, the panel were able to reach a conclusion on the various allegations.

This case highlights how important it can be to have a panel. The complainant would have been entitled to feel very disgruntled if he had not had a chance to take his complaint further to panel, but had had to continue on to the Local Government Ombudsman. For many people it would simply be too much to take that further step and they would give up at this point, even though it might be that they had a justified complaint. Another important point this case raises is whether or not the panel has the required information to reach a conclusion. On this occasion the panel were fortunate that they were able to do so. However, in the event that the panel is dissatisfied with an investigation and cannot reach a conclusion, they have the ability to adjourn the panel, to reconvene at a later date, and ask for a further and better investigation to be undertaken.

End notes

1. In April 2006 social services was reorganised and split. Since the split took place adult social services has been joined with health and children's services with education. The system of the provision of social services is now called social care.
2. This Act inserted into the *Local Authority Social Services Act 1970*, s.7, the requirement for social services authorities to have a complaints procedure.
3. At s.26(3).
4. White Paper *Caring for People*, 1989 at para 3.1.

5. *The Pindown Experience and the Protection of Children – the Report of the Staffordshire Child Care Inquiry 1990* Levy, A, and Khan, B, Staffordshire County Council 1991.
6. *The Leicestershire Inquiry* 1992 Andrew Kirkwood QC, February 1993 and the *Inquiry into Police Investigation of Complaints of Child and Sexual Abuse in Leicestershire Children's Homes* Police Complaints Authority, February 1993.
7. LAC (91) 10 DoH.
8. Ibid, at para 12.
9. SI 309 2009 the *Local Authority Social Services and National Health Service Complaints (England) Regulations*, DoH. For the importance of this split see further below.
10. [1994] 1 FLR 203 at 211.
11. [1986] 1 WLR 477 at 485.
12. [1997] 2 FCR 357. For further consideration of this case, at first instance, see C Williams *R v. Birmingham City Council, ex parte A: An unsuitable case for judicial review?* (1998) 10 Child Family Law Quarterly 89. The first instance decision was confirmed on appeal to the Court of Appeal.
13. (1996) 40 BMLR 137. For a recent pertinent example discussing whether judicial review was the appropriate remedy, rather than the complaints procedure see *R (on the application of JL and another) v. Islington London Borough Council* [2009] EWHC 458 (Admin).
14. SI 1738 2006 *The Children Act 1989 Representations Procedure (England) Regulations 2006*, reg 9. The exception to this rule is where it would not be reasonable to expect the complainant to have made the complaint within the time limit and where it is still possible to consider the complaint effectively and fairly.
15. For further consideration of remedies under the complaints procedure, see Chapter 5.
16. See case example 2 for an illustration of a very poor investigation, where none of the complainant's complaints were upheld.
17. SI 2009 309, reg 14.
18. See s.26(3)(d).
19. Another overlap example includes one where the complaint by an adult is that he has been turned down as a foster carer or as an adopter for a particular child.

Chapter 2

The Constitution of the Panel

The issues to be considered in this chapter are: How the panel is appointed; who will chair the panel; who will fulfil the role of wing members of the panel; the independence of the members of the panel and any training they may require to fulfil their role.

Composition

The composition of the panel was initially subject to a relatively low level of regulation. The *Complaints Procedures Directions*[1] section 2(1) and the *Children and Young Persons Representations Procedure Regulation* 8(3)[2] simply stated that the panel should consist of three people and include at least one independent person. Guidance stated that the independent person should chair the panel.[3] However, changes were introduced by the new regulations implemented on the 1 September 2006.[4] These regulations specify in more detail the composition of a review panel. All three members of the panel must now be independent of the authority.[5]

Somewhat surprisingly, the *Children Act Regulation* 8(5)(b)[6] allowed for the independent panel member to be the same individual as the independent person at Stage 2 of the procedure, although the *Children Act Guidance* volume 4[7] advised caution in this respect. Under the 2006 regulations this is now specifically forbidden.[8]

Chairs of the review panel

The role of the chair is crucial to the good running of the panel and to understanding the issues that can be raised with regards to the constitution of the panel. Previous guidance did not clearly state exactly what was the role of the chair. However, it is something that has developed over time. Further, in 1998 the National Complaints Officers Group produced a good practice guide on review panels that helped to clarify the procedure of a review panel and this included the role of the chair.[9] The Local Government Ombudsman has also made reference to this guidance as a model of good practice in a number of investigation reports. In the guidance accompanying the 2006 procedures there is further guidance as to the role of the chair.[10]

Taking together the various sources of guidance the main responsibilities of the chair, arising up to and on the day of the panel, can be summarised as including:[11]

- conferring with the complaints manager about the specific needs of the complainant

- agreeing who will attend as the local authority representative[12] and requesting the attendance of any other persons who may assist in understanding the complaint and its context

- taking responsibility for controlling the events of the day, ensuring the panel runs smoothly

- in consultation with the other panellists, ensuring that the pre-meeting deliberations are of sufficient length to ensure appropriate consideration of the complaint and to help enable the panel to reach its conclusions

- explaining the procedure to the parties involved – in particular the role that each of the three panel members will have in deciding the review

- ensuring that there is equal access to the documents presented to, and considered by, the panel

- ensuring that plain English is used and that everyone is given an opportunity to express themselves as well as to respond to statements made

- facilitating discussion which is productive and meaningful

- operating flexibly in response to the individual needs of each panel

- ensuring that inappropriate behaviour is challenged and that all participants are treated with respect throughout the process [see case example 1 for an illustration of where the chair needed to exercise her authority to ensure that this happened]

- ensuring that the complaint is heard in full

- after the main hearing, usually leading on the discussion and consideration of the evidence and writing the recommendations of the panel[13]

- ensuring that any disagreements of position among the panellists are recorded and seeking to reach a majority decision where necessary[14]

- managing the panel's deliberations to produce a timely and full response to the complainant and local authority within five working days of the panel meeting

- being available to meet local authority staff, if needed, after the panel meeting to discuss any recommendations arising.

It is important for the complaints manager to have a clear understanding of the role of the chair, as he will usually attend panels and be called upon to guide chairs as to their responsibilities should the need arise.[15]

Although the decision to appoint a particular chair is often done by the complaints manager in the complaints unit, it does not have to be done this way. Other ways of doing this are to use an agency for independent people or to leave it to the legal department of the authority. The disadvantage of the complaints manager not appointing the chair is that he does not then know the chair's background. Therefore, when the chair is being used for the first time he does not know if he has the ability to chair such a meeting[16] [see case example 2 for the importance of making sure that the chair is suitably qualified].

Chairs must, of course, be independent. However, there are different views as to what might constitute independence and as to what are the necessary skills for chairing the panel. One way of seeking chairs is to appoint people who are considered to be champions of a particular service user group, such as Age Concern and MIND.[17] Support for this approach can be found in the guidance,[18] which encourages consideration to be given to a member of a voluntary organisation. Furthermore, importantly, the Local Government Ombudsman sees no problem with this.

However, a note of caution should be entered regarding the possible danger this could pose. It is possible to question using individuals representing particular interest groups. It could be argued that a chair appointed in this way might use the panel to the point of finding in favour of the complainant, even where there has not been any real complaint that the department are not following accepted procedures. There could be a temptation to do this if the chair considers that the procedures do not live up to the expectations of the particular interest group from which they are drawn. Chairs do need to be vigilant in being scrupulously balanced in their approach. [See case study 3 for a possibly inappropriate approach by a chair.]

There is a real problem in achieving a balance between empowering a complainant by providing a chair with specialist expertise and having a fair panel hearing for all parties. Ultimately it would seem that the emphasis should be on chairs having a working knowledge of issues, such as disability and mental health problems, rather than necessarily having first hand working knowledge. Good practice in achieving this when recruiting panel members might be to undertake recruitment drives on the same lines as that for a full time job. Advertisements can be placed in the local press and then candidates interviewed in order to select appropriate people. This way authorities can reach an interesting cross section of people with different skills and life experiences. However, clearly this approach requires a level of financial support, which not all complaints managers will have for recruiting new chairs.

It can be argued that a social care background is an excellent pre-requisite for chairing. However, against this it can be said that someone who has retired or has previously worked as a social worker, might be disinclined to be seen to be criticising the work of social workers. This could then give rise to bias in favour of the department. Once again it would seem fair to say that there is no reason in principle why someone with a social care background should not be used, but it must be clear that the person can disengage herself from her previous role and act in a truly independent fashion.

Using people as chairs who have previously been elected members could also be a good option, but again could give rise to problems. It may be that the chair might, for example, have knowledge of the complainant's family, although not the complainant himself,[19] from previous council business or for coming from a family which was previously well-known to the council for being vexatious in complaining or for being 'notorious'. The chair in such a situation would be well advised to disqualify herself, as this could at least give rise to the appearance of bias, even if not actual bias, on the part of the chair.

Overall it is clear that it is not an easy task to establish what is perceived to be an independent panel chair based on the guidance and the constraints of finding available people.

Wing members of the review panel

All panels must be composed of three independent people.[20] Independent means a person who is neither a member nor an officer of the local authority to which the representations have been made, nor the spouse or civil partner of such a person.[21]

Some independent people do not wish to chair panels but there is no reason in principle why an independent person could not be an investigator in one complaint, a wing member in another and a chair in another. It could be argued that there is a potential for bias or difficulty in such circumstances, as in the role of chair or wing member the person may find they are reviewing the investigation of one of their colleagues, who has previously sat with them on a panel. However, the recruitment and maintenance of separate independent persons for all the different roles would undoubtedly add to already stretched budgets. Where people are used in dual roles the authority could potentially open itself up to criticism. But there is an obvious, and it is suggested stronger, counter argument to this being a problem. Independent people are exactly that and in effect they are no different from lawyers, who are often involved on the same side with other lawyers in one case but then in another represent opposing sides. A professional person should be able to play different roles without it causing any difficulties and should feel free to comment on and criticise the work of a colleague if necessary.

The success of an independent person as wing member can be down to how much support they are given to fulfil their role. This support can be offered by the complaints manager in terms of regular contact and feedback about their performance or about any issues they may have, as well as making sure that the information they get is clear and includes an outline of what their role is at panel. Training should also be considered.[22]

If any members of a panel do have personal knowledge of the complainant they certainly should not agree to sit on that panel and should return the papers. Furthermore, even if this is discovered at a very late stage, including after the panel has commenced, the panel should be abandoned and reconvened with a new appointment to panel [see case example 4 for an illustration].

Reflection of diversity and gender on the panel

The Community Care Policy Guidance[23] recommends that where possible the members of the panel should reflect the cultural diversity of the local area and have the appropriate expertise or experience of the subject matter. Similarly the 2006 *Guidance* advises that the local authority should consider the profile of the local population and the need for specialist skills, knowledge, or awareness regarding the complaint.[24]

This gives rise to two major problems for authorities: how to address this when there is only a limited time in which to set up the review[25] and the lack of resources to recruit new people who reflect the background of the complainant. It is not easy to achieve the desired result, either with regards to ethnicity or with gender balance. It is suggested that the emphasis needs to be more on having the panel within a reasonable time, rather than with having a particular individual on the review. However, if the complainant specifically suggests going over the time limit in order for the appropriate panel to be convened, within limits it may be acceptable to exceed the timescale. Communication is clearly the key to ascertaining the best approach. Some complainants will already be weary from the time taken to investigate and they may favour proceeding to panel without delay.

Challenges to the panel's composition

Particularly since the introduction of the *Human Rights Act 1998* consideration must be given as to the composition and independence of the whole panel. This issue was highlighted in *R (on the application of Beeson) v. Secretary of State for Health*,[26] a case which went to the Court of Appeal. The appeal was brought not by Dorset County Council (who were the defendants to an original application for judicial review), but by the Secretary of State as an interested party. He was joined in the proceedings so that he might respond to a particular argument based on Article 6 of the *European Convention on Human Rights*. Article 6(1) provides:

> In the determination of his civil rights and obligations or of any criminal charge against him, everyone is entitled to a fair and public hearing within a reasonable time by an independent and impartial tribunal established by law . . .

The issue that arose for consideration was the alleged want of independence and impartiality, which arose from the fact that the *Complaints Procedure Directions*[27] at the time only required one member of the panel to be independent and, in this particular case there was said to be only the one independent person, as two of the members of the panel were elected members. The case arose because Dorset County Council had decided that Mr Beeson had deprived himself of certain property belonging to him. However, they considered that the value of the property should be taken into account in assessing Mr Beeson's ability to pay for residential accommodation arranged for him by the Council pursuant to Part III of the *National Assistance Act 1948* fell.[28] This decision was challenged under the complaints procedure and eventually proceeded to a panel, which upheld the decision of the council. Given that local authorities have a financial interest in the outcome of their own decisions, there was a clear argument that the panel could be considered biased, as the elected members would have an interest in preserving funds. However, in deciding the question whether the decision-making process satisfied Article 6 taken as a whole, the Court of Appeal held that as the process included the option of applying for judicial review, where the complainant remained dissatisfied at the end of the process, there was no overall conflict with Article 6.

The importance of this decision is two-fold. First it is clearly a warning to authorities to make every effort to ensure that their panels do conform with all the requirements of independence, however that is defined, because if they get it wrong they are potentially liable to an action in judicial review. Secondly, and more helpfully from the authorities' perspective, it also provides some protection against unreasonable expectations as to how far an authority needs to go in ensuring that their panels are independent. It may be that a complainant might want to insist on a particular make-up of a panel, for example that it should consist of all men or that it should reflect the particular ethnicity of the complainant. Whilst it makes good sense to attempt to comply with reasonable requests, the authority may not be able to do so. In such circumstances, the *Beeson* case would certainly suggest that provided the members of the panel act in an independent fashion, it is not unreasonable for the authority to proceed with a panel despite not being able to comply with the complainant's wishes.

Payment of panel members

In the past one of the main reasons for authorities choosing to use elected members on their panels was due to the cost of the panel. The usual arrangement was for it to be considered as part of their duties as councillors, or to be claimed as part of their expenses from the council. Not surprisingly, therefore, concern has been expressed about the cost implications of using three independent people, which is now required under the new regulations. This undoubtedly puts a considerable strain on the already very tight budgets of complaints managers. No allowance or extra financial resources appear to have been considered when drawing up the new complaints system. Authorities which have previously confined themselves to paying expenses only to their panel members have not surprisingly had problems in recruitment.

The amount of money paid to panel members does vary widely across the country, ranging from mere expenses to around £500 per panel. Some authorities use agencies to supply them with their independent people and therefore have to use agency rates. The use of just one agency highlights a potential point of concern, giving rise to a very similar argument as expressed above: that where the chair knows the investigator well he could feel reluctant to criticise the investigation even when it would appear right to do so. Where the same agency is used for panel members, the possible concern is that when people know one another they will go along with whatever the more dominant person says, regardless of who is acting as chair. However, the same argument could also be raised as above when discussing the use of pools of people as both chairs and investigators. It could be said that anyone who works for an agency should be sufficiently professional in their approach to remain resolutely impartial and should be willing to criticise or disagree with a colleague where necessary. Every person who is asked to chair should be expected and able to assert their authority where necessary.

The huge difference in what authorities pay can be at least partly explained by the lack of guidance on payments. The effect in practice means that in some regions an independent person may prefer to choose to work for one authority rather than another on the basis of money. As a result the 'poorer' or less generous ones can then struggle to find suitable people to chair. Whilst clearly there are arguments in favour of payment being made, extremes such as automatically paying £500 per panel, even although the panel may end up being relatively simple and brief, mean that money is actually being taken away from the service user. There is no empirical research basis for the assumption that you have to pay more to get good people. It is clear from the research that those authorities which pay less are still managing to engage people with the relevant professional background and relevant expertise [see case examples 5 and 6 for comments on payments to panel members]. But it can make the process for appointment more arduous and prolonged than it needs to be.

Training of the review panel

Best practice would suggest that authorities consider training for their panels. However, what does the word 'training' mean? It is clear that training can range from simply providing a brief meeting with the panel beforehand, to employing a trainer either from inside the authority or outside it to go through the procedure in detail.

An ideal training package would cover at a minimum:

- chairing skills – interpersonal and analytical skills
- listening skills

- evidence based judgement

- specific services

- policies and procedures

- statutory duties and powers of social services

- confidentiality, data protection and freedom of information.

The initial department of Health guidance[29] recommends that training be provided to the chair and other panel members. Support for training can also be found in the *Children Act Guidance*,[30] when it advises that consideration should be given to the training of panel members.

Many authorities provide guidance in the form of what the role of the panel is on the day of the panel, either in written format or in a pre-panel meeting.[31] How useful this is in assisting the panel members has not been empirically tested but the Social Services Inspectorate in its inspection report of 1993[32] stated that panel members should be provided with guidance on the task, role, format, decision-making, communication of findings and access to information issues. Further the Practice Guidance[33] also states that it is recommended that training be provided for the independent role in chairing the panel, together with the other panel members. In a 2002 Local Government Ombudsman report[34] it was evident that training can be essential if the authority are to avoid the situation where:

> *most disturbing of all . . . is the fact that until now [the chair] has not understood the extent of his responsibility as an independent chair. He did not know he had the power to reject an investigation report.*

and later:

> *the council is at fault for not providing [the chair] and fellow panel members with proper support, guidance and training to enable them to carry out their responsibilities properly.*

The view of the Local Government Ombudsman Office is that training should be provided. Should a dissatisfied complainant take his case to the Local Government Ombudsman, and the Local Government Ombudsman feel the need to interview members of the panel, he would ask what information and training the panel members had had and what their understanding was of their role at panel. Somewhat alarmingly, the Local Government Ombudsman found in the particular case mentioned above that it was quite clear from correspondence that the chair of the panel simply did not understand his role and, what is more, the chair was a lawyer. This demonstrates that authorities should take nothing for granted, and simply because a person appears to be a suitable chair and does not appear to need training is not necessarily the case.

A particular concern for authorities could be the cost of training individuals who then might not be called to sit on a panel for months or even years. The view might be taken that it is simply not worth doing training, as so few panels take place. From a resources point of view this is an eminently reasonable position to adopt. Further, it is not necessarily just a question of money, but also one of time. However, lack of time or resources does not take away from the fact that all people, however experienced, cannot be expected to have detailed knowledge of all the areas for training listed above. Therefore some effort does need to be made to meet the need for panel members to be trained.

For those authorities that have a pool of independent people, which is maintained over a number of years, the use of regular meetings in order to review issues surrounding complaints is one way forward. There is also the possibility of attendance at regional or national conferences. Another suggestion is to look to explore the possibility of having a reciprocal arrangement between authorities, of acting as independent people for each other. The thinking behind this is to address the problem of not having enough money to fund training and the problem of finding people with the requisite knowledge. The different authorities could then join together for training purposes. Subcontracting training to an appropriate body is clearly another possibility. Finally, as an absolute minimum, detailed thought should be given as to what material should be sent out with the panel papers, which should include, where necessary, items such as the policies and procedures involved in the particular service, any legislative material and a guide as to how the panel should be conducted.[35]

What a panel should be looking for in a report

It is clear that the panel is heavily dependent on the investigator's report, as it sets out the complaint and the findings from the investigation. One of the panel's tasks is, therefore, to consider whether a report has been 'fair and thorough'. If there is a defective report the panel must either make findings about the issues itself, or, if this is not possible or appropriate, the panel will have to remit the complaint back for further and better investigation.

The sort of things panels should be looking for in an investigator's report are:

- Have the timescales been met? If they have not, why have they been exceeded?

- Have all the issues been addressed?

- Has the specific complaint been dealt with? Simply providing a brilliant conclusion is not enough for the panel, who must ask the question: 'Yes, but how does that answer the complaint?'

- Is the investigation comprehensive? Has it included every relevant element and recorded both sides of the case being presented?

- Have all relevant parties been interviewed and records examined? If for any reason this has not proved possible, has a proper explanation been given as to why not?

- Has all the relevant guidance, records, statutory material and so on been quoted that has led to the conclusions, and is it clear that it is quoted material?

- If local and internal procedures and guidance have been relied on, do they accurately reflect the appropriate national provisions?

- Have the 'desired outcomes' of the complainant actually been addressed, regardless of whether or not the investigator concurs with them?

- Is it clear that the report does not reflect prejudice of any kind?

- If the complainant talks about the distress caused, has this been recognised in the report?[36]

A good report should be lucid, succinct and expressed clearly. There should be clarity without omission, avoiding jargon as far as possible. The same, of course, should also be the case in the panel's final written findings.

The importance of the complaints manager

The complaints manager has a key role in making sure that the panel is representative and equipped to carry out its function. It should never be underestimated how time-consuming and difficult a job this can be for the complaints manager, as it ranges from recruiting members for panels right through to supporting and monitoring the independent people. However, at least it can be argued that complaints managers are best placed to do this recruitment, as they know the complainant and the area of the complaint and therefore are likely to have the most success in finding suitable members for the panel. However, more generally what is needed is support to assist complaints managers in advertising for suitable people and perhaps some regional or nationally led training and monitoring of those who work as an independent person.

Encouraging a dialogue between independent people and the complaints manager, particularly those who have regular meetings, can be used to flag up any issues, to raise matters for training and to establish future availability. This is a potential opportunity to bring in out-of-house training providers who can come in and speak about particular areas of interest. Used well, a range of matters, for example an annual update on recent changes in the law which may affect panels and the decisions they are making, can thereby be addressed. There could also be a dedicated website where there could be a discussion forum and a place for posting new developments.

Key points summary

- All the new regulations and guidance are to be found in *Statutory Instrument 2006 1738* and *Getting the Best from Complaints*. The adult procedures for panel can be found in *Statutory Instrument 2006 1681* and *Learning from Complaints*.

- The chair of the panel has a key role to play. She should be clear as to her duties and responsibilities.

- The chair must be scrupulously independent, not influenced by either her work background or by coming from a particular service user representation/campaigning background.

- There is no reason why the same people cannot be used in multi-functional roles. At different times a person can operate as chair, wing member, investigating officer and independent person.

- Potential members of a panel should disqualify themselves from sitting if they have prior knowledge of the complainant or complaint.

- Provided the panel is truly independent there is no requirement for a panel to be of a particular composition.

- However, wherever possible, an attempt should be made to reflect appropriate skills and/or gender balance if relevant.

- It is normal to expect panel members to be paid but a high flat rate fee is probably not necessary.

- Panel members should be trained. In order to spread the cost this may be achieved by arranging joint training with other local authorities.

- The panel will be looking for the investigating officer's report to be clear, well written and well argued, a model the panel should also strive for.

- The complaints manager plays a key role both in managing complaints and in supporting panel members.

Practice illustrations and case examples

1. The following case example raises the issue as to what should be done if an attendee at panel does not comply with the requirement of showing courtesy and respect to all attendees at panel:

   A complainant who attended panel was well known to the department and viewed as something of a troublemaker. At panel one of the members of staff sat doing things such as raising her eyebrows to heaven and shifting in her seat, showing disdain for the complainant each time he spoke. All three members of the panel became conscious of this.

   This gives rise to the issue: should the chair ignore this behaviour, speak in private to the member of staff, or say something in open session? It is suggested that the first option is not really an option. If a member of staff is behaving badly then it is up to the chair to put a stop to it; that is part of her role. Of the other two possibilities it is suggested that the better choice of the two is to say something in open session. The reason for this is that if all the panel members are picking up highly negative vibes emanating from a member of staff, it is extremely likely that the complainant will receive the same message too. If nothing is said publicly, the message that the complainant will get is both that the panel are happy to tolerate this and, much more importantly, if the panel does not uphold any of the complaints it could be said it was because the panel were influenced by this unspoken behaviour. It is therefore important to speak about this to the member of staff in front of everyone and to warn him that if he continues he will have to be asked to leave.

2. The importance of having a strong chair, who is capable of confronting others should he feel that their behaviour is not appropriate,[37] is illustrated by the following quotation from an interview with one of the chairs in the research:

   I had a panel recently where, as she walked in, one panel member said 'I am already biased against the complainant'. I did manage to talk her around a bit prior to the panel and she sort of accepted that perhaps she should not be as biased. The other member, the minute the hearing had ended, said he was biased against him [the complainant] because he had not turned up. So, either he had not read the papers or had not read them properly, as they stated that the complainant found it difficult to deal with such a meeting and that that was why he was not coming but sending someone to represent him. I then had to spend time explaining this. In the end both panel members did behave sensibly, but it was a bit of a struggle to get them there.

3. It is very important that in recruitment any potentially biased approach is tested. The possibility that a chair with a particular interest may not approach panels in a suitably unbiased fashion is illustrated by the following quotation by one of the chairs in the research:

   They asked the voluntary groups to go to a meeting at the Town Hall. I have always been involved in putting forward the point of view of the disabled. Anything where you can put across the word of those with disabilities then I get involved and put the message across.

   Although this chair may well have been suitably disinterested when it came to adjudicating at the panel, the worry is that this might not be the case if the complainant was disabled.

4. The requirement that all panel members pay careful attention to the need for complete independence is illustrated by the following example:

   A complaint was made by a foster parent who was challenging the decision not to fund alterations to her home. The complainant had attended the panel and the panel had gone through all of the issues and were close to the point of retiring to consider their findings and recommendations. However, at this point one of the panellists, a councillor,[38] realised she had previously dealt with a request from the complainant at planning committee, when the foster parent had applied for permission to extend her house. After taking legal advice, it was decided that the planning decision was so closely linked with the substance of the complaint that it must result in the panel having to be abandoned.

5. In the research it was found that only three authorities did not pay more than expenses. The problem of limiting payments in such a way was illustrated by one respondent who commented:

   We do get some eligible people who slip through. We had one lady who approached us but when we told her that we don't pay she already had her foot out the door and her coat on.

   It is not unreasonable to expect to pay someone a sum of money when it is possible they may have to spend many hours not just at the panel, but also in preparing for the panel and in formulating the panel's response to what might be a complicated case.

6. However, although payment might reasonably be expected, some panels are relatively simple and only take a short time to complete. At the other end of the scale of payment, one respondent commented:

[Our chairs] get paid £250 pre-panel preparation, which is to read the papers to understand it and raise any issues in advance, and they get £250 for appearance on the day. I think it says something about our commitment in terms of getting quality people and paying them well. These are the kind of people who will not get out of bed for a cheese sandwich. It always kind of knocks people back when I say how much it is. On a complicated complaints case people can spend a considerable amount of time reading a lot of papers and understanding articulate debates within that. Precious time is much valued.

It may be that this complaints manager would be well advised to spend some money on advertising for further panel chairs. Although in the short term this could cost money, it seems likely that in the long run that payment based the actual amount of time spent, rather than a simple flat fee, would work out financially cheaper. 'Quality people' do not necessarily charge large sums of money!

End notes

1. *Complaints Procedures Directions 1990* issued under s.7B (3) of the *Local Authority Social Services Act 1970* amended by s.50 of the *NHS and Community Care Act 1990*.
2. *Children and Young Persons Representations Procedure (Children) Regulations 1991* (SI 1991 No. 894).
3. *Community Care Policy Guidance*, HMSO (1991) Annex A, Para 4.
4. SI 2006 No 1738.
5. SI 2006 No 1738, reg 19. The regulations are different for adults, where at least two members must be independent and the third cannot be either an officer of the authority or their spouse or civil partner. The chair must be an independent person: SI 2006 No 1681, reg. 12.
6. Vol. 3, Department of Health, HMSO 1991.
7. HMSO 1991 at para 5.33.
8. SI 2006 No 1738, reg. 19(3).
9. *Complaints Review Panels – A Good Practice Guide* (1998), National Complaints Officers Group, Hamilton Training Service, Stoke on Trent.
10. *Getting the Best from Complaints*, Annex 1, Definitions of Roles.
11. This does not claim to be an exhaustive list, as unexpected events can always arise at panel, throwing fresh responsibility onto the chair. However, the list does cover the major areas.
12. This is included as it appears in the guidance. However, it seems very unlikely that in practice this will happen. The complaints manager is the person who knows who to contact to ensure that the appropriate person represents the authority. There is no reason to suppose that the chair will be in a position to be able to make such a judgement.
13. Although this is discussed later in Chapter 5, under 'A record of the outcome'.
14. See Chapter 5 for unanimous or majority decisions.
15. Further discussed below.
16. This has further implications where there is no training provided, see below. And see case example 2 for the importance of making sure that the chair is suitably qualified.

Complaints Panels in Social Care © Catherine Williams and Katy Ferris 2010 www.russellhouse.co.uk

17. This was recommended early on in the life of the procedure – see *The Right to Complain: Practice Guidance on Complaints Procedures in Social Services Departments.* DoH & SSI London: HMSO 1991 Para 4.22.

18. *The Children Act 1989 Guidance and Regulations Volume 4.* HMSO 1991, at para 5.33.

19. As if the chair actually knew the complainant she would automatically have to disqualify herself from hearing the complaint.

20. SI 2006 No 1738, reg. 19(2).

21. *Getting the Best from Complaints* para 3.13.1 and, as noted above, the independent person appointed to Stage 2 may not be a member of the panel (reg 19(3)).

22. This is discussed later in this chapter.

23. HMSO (1991) Annex A, Para 2 supported by the DoH Practice Guidance Para 4.23 *The Right to Complain* 1991.

24. *Getting the Best from Complaints*, para 3.13.2.

25. Which is 30 working days: see SI 1738, reg 19(4).

26. [2002] EWCA Civ 1812.

27. *Complaints Procedure Directions* 1990.

28. Ss 21(2A) and (2B).

29. *The Right to Complain: Practice Guidance on Complaints Procedures in Social Services Departments.* DoH London: HMSO 1991, at para 8.11.

30. *The Children Act 1989 Guidance and Regulations.* DoH London: HMSO 1991, at para 5.34.

31. For discussion of the pre-panel meeting see below, Chapter 4.

32. *The Inspection of Complaints Procedures in Local Authority Social Services Departments*, SSI DoH HMSO July 1993.

33. *The Right to Complain: Practice Guidance on Complaints Procedures in Social Services Departments*, at para 8.13. DoH & SSI London: HMSO 1991.

34. *Report on an Investigation into Complaint No 01/C/09018 against Wolverhampton City Council* LGO: Coventry

35. As discussed further in Chapter 3.

36. As the panel has to consider the question of maladministration and compensation, it is important that this is specifically addressed. See further Chapter 5, which deals with types of recommendations and remedies.

37. And see Chapter 4, case examples 1B and 1C, for further illustrations of th s point.

38. At the time of the case a councillor was permitted to sit.

Chapter 3

Arrangements for the Panel Hearing

This chapter considers the actions which need to be taken prior to the day of the panel. It covers the timescales that need to be met when making arrangements; examines what information should be provided to those attending the panel and considers the possible venues for the hearing.

Timescales

The complainant has 20 working days in which to request to move to a panel hearing after receiving the Stage 2 response.[1] Having received such a request, the guidance stipulates that the authority should acknowledge such request in writing within two days of receiving it.[2] The guidance acknowledges that it is a complainant's right to proceed to panel, but then rather oddly follows this up by saying that 'the complaints manager should assess requests for the review panel as they are presented on a case by case basis'.[3] It is not immediately evident what this means. The view of the Local Government Ombudsman is that the complaints manager is entitled to express an opinion that the complainant should not take the complaint any further but the Ombudsman's position is clear. There is a statutory procedure that should be gone through if the complainant wants it. Although there are complaints that will not get resolved by going to panel, if the complainant says they want to progress then they have nowhere else to go to but to review and they are therefore entitled to go.

The question arises: what should happen if the complainant either delays asking for a panel beyond 30 days, but has an explanation for the delay, or fails to request within the timescale but is then particularly vigorous in his demand for a panel? The guidance makes no reference as to what should happen should the complainant so delay, but this is something commented on by the Local Government Ombudsman. Furthermore, delay on the part of the authority in moving to panel after a request is an issue which may be examined if the complainant proceeds to the Local Government Ombudsman. The Local Government Ombudsman takes the view that there are sometimes very good reasons for a complainant not having responded within the timescale, it may be perfectly reasonable. The authority should therefore respond positively and set up a panel, unless the time lag is so extreme that there can be no possible justification for it. Authorities should be particularly generous in extending the timescale in the case of a child complainant. Equally, the ombudsman takes the view that if an authority have not managed to set up a panel within the timescale, provided reasons are given for any delay this is not something for which the authority are liable to be criticised. Essentially it is only unnecessary, avoidable delay that would give rise to an adverse finding.

Under the previous regulations[4] the panel was required to meet within 28 days of a request to have the hearing. Achieving this deadline did prove to be problematic: one commonplace reason being that staff did not give attendance a high priority. Some authorities found that it could take three to six months to arrange. Clearly then, as now, this was unacceptable in view of the statutory time limits. The time limit under the new regulations is now 30 working days.[5] Should any authority find that arranging a panel within the timescale is being hampered due to a lack of serious commitment to the process then, at the very least, the director, or other suitably highly placed and authoritative individual, should issue an instruction to all staff reminding them of the necessity of making attendance at panels a priority in their diaries. Breach of the time limit due to it being a low priority would clearly not be an acceptable reason should a case proceed on to the Local Government Ombudsman and could lead to a finding of maladministration.

Best practice would dictate that if there are any delays or developments with the arrangements for the panel the complaints manager, or other relevant individual, should keep the complainant informed. If authorities fail to keep complainants informed they are likely to become increasingly unhappy and less likely to tolerate any later excuses if anything else goes wrong. However, valid delays may arise for any number of reasons. These reasons include: attempting to get hold of all the right personnel; getting the complainant to commit to a date and selecting a panel that is reflective of race and/or gender, although, as discussed in the previous chapter, trying to achieve best practice in terms of having a balanced panel can mean that time limits are increasingly difficult to achieve. In research conducted by Bridge[6] it was said that, from the perspective of complaints managers, they are always expected to work to unrealistic time-scales, experiencing pressure from the many actors involved, each with their own agenda. Indeed, the complaints manager, even before this stage, can become something of a peacekeeper between the various parties involved.

Delay taken in arranging the panel was an issue in a Local Government Ombudsman report,[7] where the request to proceed to panel was made in March 1999 and the panel finally took place in December 1999. Although there were faults on both the complainant's side and that of the council, the Local Government Ombudsman found that the delay, along with the overall treatment of the complainant's issues, was unsatisfactory and amounted to maladministration due to the consequent injustice of prolonged uncertainty and distress.[8]

In another report, the Local Government Ombudsman stressed the need to keep the complainant informed of any delay.[9] At paragraph 13 the Local Government Ombudsman stated:

> Whilst I find it understandable that officers might take the view that their normal work should take precedence over a complaint about events that happened some time before, the council has a duty to comply with the statutory timescales.

Another consequence of delay in arranging a panel is that it is possible that it might limit the capacity of the panel to speak to the pertinent people involved and resolve the issues, as people within the authority retire or move on to other positions. If people with relevant knowledge are no longer available to attend the panel this obviously hampers the panel in its deliberations.

Delay and priority of those in attendance

One way of attempting to resolve the problem of delay is to set a priority order for those who should be present at panel. A useful method is to check with the complainant first, then the chair and then move down the list, with the staff being the last to be told. This, clearly, will only work in authorities where there is a strong ethos that staff must make themselves available and fit around the requirements of the complainant. However, another method which can be used in authorities where the complaints managers feels that the authority does not have a culture of giving complaints a high priority is to make sure that the date is one which could be made by the staff first, as they need to be there.[10] However, there are dangers with such an approach as was shown in a report by the Local Government Ombudsman[11] [see case example 1 for an example of an incorrect approach to the setting up of panels]. The complainant pointed out that nobody had contacted him to organise a date for the panel which would be suitable for him. A panel was organised involving eight other people and then it was discovered that the complainant was not available that day. Consequently, because of the requirement to hold the panel meeting within twenty-eight days of it being agreed, the complainant had only three days notice of the meeting and papers he had prepared for the panel members to read were delivered to them only on the morning of the meeting itself. This was one of the deficiencies that led to a payment of £500 to the complainant for his time and trouble in bringing the complaint.

Whichever method is chosen, once a date is found within or as close to the 30-day timescale as possible and it has been communicated to those required to attend, staff in particular should commit themselves to attending the hearing unless positively prevented by unforeseen circumstances.

The Local Government Ombudsmans take the view that it is understandable that people who are required to attend or to sit on the panel can be very busy and it can therefore be difficult to sort out when the panel can take place. Therefore, it is not so much delay in meeting the deadline that would be concerning, but more any lack of feedback given to the complainant as to where they are in the process. The Local Government Ombudsman respects the fact that some councils experience difficulty and although they do have concerns about delay right the way through the whole complaints system, this is because they consider the timescales can be unrealistic, as they simply cannot be met.

The timescale for establishing panels was considered in *R v. Barnet London Borough Council, ex parte P*[12] where there had been a clear breach of Regulation 8(4).[13] Judge Jackson decided to give the local authority the opportunity to establish a panel, as he considered that suitable persons who had enough time to prepare for the hearing must constitute the panel. The case involved a 17 year-old boy who was receiving services from the local authority for his disabilities. The boy's parents raised a number of complaints under the complaints procedure which were not dealt with until some considerable time had passed. The parents were not satisfied with the response of the local authority and asked for a panel hearing. They then proceeded to judicial review. Having seen the history of past complaints, Jackson J said that he feared that the complaints procedure 'may not lead to an early and amicable resolution of the dispute'. However, he expressed the hope that this complaint, now being limited to a single issue, would be dealt with more speedily and within the time limits. Jackson J, in discussing the time limits laid down for resolving complaints, said that whether they are mandatory or directory was not something he had to decide or indeed would decide. In the subsequent case of *Re P (Children Act 1989, ss22 and 26)*,[14] Charles J decided that, in reviewing the provisions of the *Children Act* sections

22, 23 and 26 and the regulations, the timescales are directory rather than mandatory. This would have the effect that non compliance with timescales would be treated as an irregularity, rather than rendering any decision taken being deemed void. To hold otherwise would clearly only set back the complaint being resolved and defeat the aims of the complaints procedure. As a consequence of this decision, the sanction is that the authority may be penalised for not complying with timescales, but no more than that.

Delays in setting up a panel have also been the subject of reference to the Ombudsman. In August 2004 the Local Government Ombudsman reported on a complaint against Sheffield City Council.[15] The complaint was made on behalf of a man with learning difficulties and an autistic spectrum disorder. His brother, Mr Hill, complained that the Council failed to assess his brother's needs properly in 2000 and then failed to re-assess his needs as recommended by a review panel. He also complained that the Council failed to assess his own needs as his brother's carer, failed to provide his brother with an adequate service, and failed to deal properly with complaints about these matters. The report states:[16]

> The solicitor wrote on 25 September 2001 requesting the matter be put to a review panel. A hearing was arranged for 26 November 2001, but was postponed because the solicitor was ill.
>
> No action appears to have been taken by the Council to rearrange the hearing despite reminders from the solicitor in January and April 2002. The hearing was eventually rearranged for 14 June 2002.

The Ombudsman found that the complaints were justified and upheld the complaint from Mr Hill about the way the complaint had been handled, including the time delay and the failure to implement the recommendations of the panel to carry out a re-assessment of the service users' needs. She concluded that both parties had suffered the injustice of a loss of support for several years and made a number of recommendations in order to remedy this injustice, including the payment of compensation for loss of service. The Council subsequently agreed to abide by the recommendations, including making a payment of a compensatory award amounting to a total of £6,000, in accordance with the recommendation by the Local Government Ombudsman.

Postponement of the panel by the complainant

In view of the requirement that the local authority should set the panel up within 30 days, if the complainant wishes to delay the panel the local authority will need to know the reasons for such delay. One problem that could then arise is if the complainant asks the complaints manager to postpone the complainant's right to go to panel in order for the complainant to seek legal advice about the complaint. What should the complaints manager do if the complainant makes it known that he might then seek legal redress dependent on that legal advice? Should he delay setting up a panel hearing in order, potentially, to assist the complainant in bringing other proceedings against the authority, which may take a considerable time, or should he go ahead within the timescale? The Local Government Ombudsman's view is that although the complainant should be allowed to do that, there would have to be a cut-off point and the complaints manager would need to get some kind of a timescale from the complainant. However, in keeping with the regulations surrounding bringing a complaint initially, where the complainant notifies the authority in writing of his intention to bring legal proceedings that would give the authority the right to refuse to set up a panel hearing.[17]

Generally speaking, where the complainant returns for a review after a considerable lapse of time, consideration should be given to going ahead with a panel where the complainant is very insistent. The complainant normally has to bring his initial complaint no later than one year after the grounds for making the complaint have arisen, but these limits can be extended in appropriate cases.[18] In similar fashion, authorities should consider carefully the particular circumstances of the case if there is a delay in requesting a panel. They should not have a blanket policy of refusing such a request. This would be fettering their discretion and could lead to a finding of maladministration against them. Furthermore, if a complainant delays in asking for a panel and then the local authority take in excess of the 30 days to establish one, the Local Government Ombudsman, if subsequently complained to, would take a sympathetic view of the local authority's delay.

The provision of information prior to panel

Guidance provides that the papers for a panel hearing should go out at least 10 working days in advance of the hearing[19] [see case example 2 for the importance of making sure that the correct papers are sent out]. Similarly, the National Complaints Officers Group Guide[20] gives a preferred target of 10–14 days. In practice this target may be hard to meet due to the shortness of time for setting up the panel.

The importance of sending out papers well in advance arises because panel members inevitably have other demands on their time. If papers are sent out late, panel members are likely to struggle to read and digest the papers properly prior to the panel. Not infrequently there is a considerable amount of material. Time is needed to go through the papers, giving the panel members an opportunity to understand the issues fully and to start formulating questions before getting to the panel. If there is a delay in sending out papers, this obviously has implications for the day of the panel. The panel members may fail to ask the right questions or miss items of importance due to lack of adequate preparation time. Furthermore, if papers are late in coming out and the chair has concerns about the length of time that has been set aside for the panel, it is very late in the day for the chair to be expressing those concerns [see case study 3 for a consideration of how much time should be set aside for the hearing].

In considering the provision of information, the guidance stresses on a number of occasions the need for members of the panel to be bound by the normal rules of confidentiality.[21] From this, it follows that the papers generated for the panel should only be distributed to those who are expected to attend and then anyone else on a strictly need-to-know basis. There is no official guidance for complaints manager to follow as to who this might be. However, the non-attendees who might 'need to know' will include, for example, the local authority's legal section, if queries have been raised and it is felt necessary to seek legal advice in advance of the panel.

Information for the panel members

In order to fulfil their role the panel members need to have all the relevant information to enable them to draw conclusions about the complaint. The guidance provides that the members of the panel will normally need to have access to: information on Stage 1 (as relevant), the Stage 2 investigation report(s), the local authority's adjudication, any policy, practice or guidance information relevant to the complaint, and any comments that the complainant has submitted to the panel. The papers should also include information on any local practice around panels, such as conduct, roles and responsibilities.'[22] Good practice would dictate that somewhere in the papers the reasons for the complainant remaining dissatisfied after Stage 2 should be included.

Ideally all information will be supplied in the panel papers sent out in advance. However, if last minute items are provided, this gives rise to a problem. Not infrequently it is the complainant who turns up at panel with extra information. In these circumstances it is best left up to the panel chair to decide whether or not to accept the information. As a general rule of thumb it is better to accept such material. However, this should be subject to a limit on the amount that can be accepted last minute. Clearly if the complainant comes to panel with a Lever Arch file full of material, it is not possible to read and digest such material on the day of the panel. It would not be reasonable to expect the panel to agree to include it. The Local Government Ombudsman takes the view that if the complainant brings new information to the panel, the chair has three choices. She can scrutinise it there and then and accept it; she can adjourn the panel; or she can reject it. It can be a hard decision for the chair to make but somebody has to take it and it is up to the chair to decide which is the most appropriate course of action. A different, more restrictive, view may be adopted if it is the department which submits late information. They should be more organised than the complainant and know how the system operates. Consequently there is less reason to accept a late submission of material, although, of course, it can be that it is acceptable. Once again it is up to the chair, who simply needs to exercise her discretion sensibly in the particular circumstances.

The actual arrangement of the panel papers is also an issue, as they can be difficult to follow. Some authorities start off the papers in reverse order, which means moving backwards through the complaint. This can cause confusion and gives particular cause for concern if the complainant consequently gains a bad impression and considers that the chair does not know what is going on. The arrangement of papers clearly needs thinking about, but ideally it seems clear that, after a basic introduction outlining the key issues, most people would prefer to have the papers ordered by date, starting with the earliest contact with the complaints unit, rather than in reverse order. If all material with dates is supplied in this fashion, material such as policies and local practices can then be in the appendices, again if relevant in date order, and clearly labelled as to what they are [see case example 4 for an illustration of this problem].

Information given to the complainant

The guidance stipulates that the same panel papers should be sent to all attendees at panel. However, many areas say they give 'all relevant materials' to the complainant. So, the question arises as to what amounts to 'relevant materials'? This will clearly depend on the complaints manager, or other person compiling the panel papers. Questions can arise as to whether, for example, telephone records or internal e-mails between staff should be supplied. This probably should be left to the discretion of the complaints manager; it would be difficult to lay down a blanket rule, but what is clear is that the complainant should not be left in the position whereby all other attendees are privy to relevant information but he is not.

In the original guidance accompanying the procedure it is recommended as good practice that the complainant be informed of the names and status of the panel members in advance.[23] Although this is not specifically mentioned in the more recent guidance, when sending out the panel papers the names of the chair and the two wing members should be on the papers for the complainant to see. This is important, as is notifying the complainant of any last minute changes, as it is possible that someone might be unwittingly sitting on the panel who is known to the complainant and to whom he might therefore object [see case example 5 for consideration of this point].

Knowledge of who will be sitting on a panel was an issue in a Local Government Ombudsman report in which a complainant specifically raised the fact that he had not been informed of the people to be on the panel as a complaint, as well as a claim that he had not received information about how the panel would operate.[24] It is clearly important that complainants, as with the panel members themselves, have the opportunity to notify the complaints manager if they have had previous involvement with any of the people attending the panel and if they feel, for genuine reasons, that the people on the panel will not be appropriate to hear their argument.

It is also important that the complainant is given information about how the complaints procedure operates, at whatever stage they are at. Failure to do so led to a Local Government Ombudsman report in which criticism was made of an authority which had failed to provide details of the complaints procedure to the complainant, despite a clear request to that effect having been made.[25]

Venue and timing of the panel

Very little guidance is given as to the location or setting of panels. The guidance simply provides that panels should be provided locally and with due regard to the complainant's availability and convenience.[26] Many authorities use buildings such as the town hall/civic centre/city hall; others use a variety of social services, or council buildings; and others attempt to use neutral venues.

Both the previous and present guidance suggest that the panel meeting should be as informal as possible.[27] Additionally, according to the National Complaints Officers Guidance 'large formal committee rooms are not considered suitable for this purpose.'[28] It may therefore be inappropriate to use places such as the town hall, which could be extremely off-putting to a nervous complainant. However, contra to this, the use of a formal setting can be justified on the basis that people like the opportunity to come to a municipal building to make their complaint, because it is their day in court. The building provides an authenticity to the day from their point of view. In light of this contradictory view, good practice would suggest that the person arranging the panel should contact the complainant about a venue, not in terms of the complainant actually choosing the venue, but in order to check the suitability of both location and setting. In this way due regard can be given to the convenience of the location in terms of travel to and from the venue, suitability for the type of complainant and accessibility for those with mobility or other difficulties.[29]

Under normal circumstances it is not acceptable to limit either the location or the timing of a panel too restrictively, as the limiting of time and place could be open to challenge, probably by further reference to the Local Government Ombudsman or possibly an application for judicial review. The guidance clearly implies that in practice the authority would not meet the administrative standards that have been set, that is that panels 'should be provided locally and with due regard to the complainant's availability and convenience' [see case example 1 on this]. It would seem very likely, therefore, that the Local Government Ombudsman would regard it as maladministration on the part of the authority should an attempt be made to put restrictive limits on when and where panels take place. More tricky, but possible, is the argument that it might leave the authority open to an action in judicial review. It could be argued that the guidance implies that such an action is possible, as it opens the door to saying that complainants have a 'legitimate expectation' that panels will be local and convenient. If this requirement is breached, it gives rise to grounds for argument in judicial review.

It may be possible to limit the panel, however, in exceptional circumstances. Where the complainant persists in submitting a surfeit of material, far in excess of that which reasonably could be expected to be considered by the panel, and quite possibly complaining not simply about the action of the department but also about that of various other organisations, the panel may be justified in limiting the amount of time available to the complainant. Should this difficulty arise the department would be well advised to check with the Local Government Ombudsman's office first to confirm that the office thinks such action potentially reasonable.

A fairly commonplace issue that might need to be taken into account in the setting up of panels is that of childcare. Good practice would suggest that attempts should be made to assist, if that is an issue. Also, if the complainant has particular restrictions placed upon him as he is, for example, in jail or on a curfew, efforts must be made to provide a solution to such a difficulty. This could be done by contacting the prison to see if a panel could be held within it or setting up a video link. Having a relaxed setting, with refreshments available, is another issue that authorities need to be concerned about.

It clearly makes sense to check out venues in advance. In the research undertaken by one of the authors there was one complaints manager who provided an 'awful warning' for all. The example was given of the following experience, where the attempt had been made to go further afield than the usual council buildings used and where the complaints manager learnt of the need to be careful to make sure the venue is appropriate:

We have learnt from one panel where we booked a community centre and we didn't go to check it out in advance. I can't believe that I didn't, but when we got there it was like a big hall which had been divided down the middle so it wasn't confidential. There was a slimming club weigh-in on the other side, with shouts of 'Suzanne ten pounds!' for example. So we got up and moved and shuffled around. We always check the venues out now. I was appalled that I hadn't [see also case example 6].

The venue for the panel is not just a matter of how appropriate it may be, but finding an appropriate venue may add to the delay and cost of a panel. This is a further factor that the complaints manager has to bear in mind. If the venue chosen is a social services' building, the cost to the complaints budget is likely to be considerably less than it will be for many other venues. If operating under very stringent financial constraints, it is no wonder that cost is a factor which affects decision-making. Additionally, the justified argument can be made, particularly where the complaint is about refusal of a service or lack of resources, that money should not be wasted on more expensive venues than is necessary. If finding a suitable venue is going to cause delay, pressure may be on in order to convene the panel within the 30-day time limit.

The complainant's home

The Local Government Ombudsman's view on whether it is appropriate to hold a panel in the complainant's home is that this would be acceptable if the complainant could not travel, but it certainly should not be held in a panel member's house. However, holding a panel in the home is likely to be difficult, as it probable that there will not really be enough space. Should this be a problem the solution might be for the complaints manager and the panel to meet the complainant in the home, with an advocate present, and then for everyone to reconvene in an appropriate location, with the advocate but minus the complainant. This is not ideal but is probably the best compromise that can be suggested.

Despite the possibility of holding the panel in the complainant's home, best practice would suggest that where possible holding the panel in the home should be avoided. A better solution is to try and be creative on locations. Although panels are not meant to be highly formal, the panel being held in the complainant's home does not reflect the appropriate level of seriousness that a panel should operate under. Also, although the complainant will necessarily have invited people into the home, he will be vulnerable to an invasion of his privacy and it will make it more difficult for the panel to maintain a distance and independence from the complainant than holding a panel elsewhere would. An alternative to the complainant's home, where it seems to be the only option, is to follow the example given above of taking the whole panel to the home, or simply to have the chair meet with the complainant at home along with the complaints manager and an advocate or support person to talk through what the complainant wishes to complain about. Then they could meet with the rest of the panel attendees at a suitable meeting room nearby.

Overall administrative arrangements

The importance of the administrative arrangements prior to the panel are not to be underestimated as they may form part of a complaint to the Local Government Ombudsman and, combined with other errors, may result in a finding of maladministration. An example of this arose in an investigation into the London Borough of Bromley[30] where the complainant had contacted the local authority to complain about the composition of the panel; the council's failure to offer a pre-meeting to explain the procedure; the council's failure to provide support and assistance; and the council's failure to advise of the start time of the hearing. The Local Government Ombudsman did not find that, in themselves, these individual issues formed maladministration but that they were a part of the wider complaint, which did amount to maladministration.

Key points summary

- The complainant has 20 working days in which to request a panel after receiving the Stage 2 response.

- If the complainant delays beyond this time, the authority should exercise its discretion in deciding whether or not to hold a panel. More leeway should be given to child complainants.

- The authority has 30 days in which to hold the panel after receipt of the complainant's request.

- Considerable breach of the time limit, without a valid reason, could lead to a finding of maladministration.

- There should be a clear system of priorities in making arrangements for attendance at panel. The complainant's availability is probably the best starting point.

- Panel papers should be sent out at least 10 working days in advance of the panel.

- If there are late submissions to the papers, the chair should decide whether or not to permit their inclusion.

- The complainant should be informed of the identity of the chair and wing members.

- The complaints manager should ensure the suitability for the complainant of both the venue and timing of the panel.

- Should the administrative arrangements for the panel be defective, this could lead to a finding of maladministration.

Practice illustrations and case examples

1. It is important that the complainant's availability is checked when first setting up the panel. One respondent had a very restrictive system as the following illustrates:

   They don't get much choice about the time as we have been told by the director that it is 6 p.m. on a Thursday. Unless someone came up with an incredible excuse for not having it on that day and time, I would be reluctant to change it. Most of our panels the complainant does not turn up.

   Quite apart from the manifest breach of the procedure in limiting panels in this way, another feature of this comment is the statement that most complainants do not attend. This should set alarm bells ringing with any panel, who should make rigorous enquiries if this is a feature of a case. Unless the complainant has requested it, to continue with the panel would almost certainly amount to maladministration.

2. The complaints unit needs to be meticulous in the process of sending out information prior to panel. The dangers of not being meticulous are illustrated by the following example:

    A complainant had made a whole series of complaints, including one alleging a serious breach of confidentiality. A panel was duly set up and the papers sent out. The complaints unit used a template on which was written certain basic information. However, in accordance with standard practice, the template was amended from one complaint to another. On this occasion the unit failed to delete the previous complainant's name and address but went on to include all the other material of the complaint. The unit then sent out the material to the previous complainant. Fortunately the previous complainant realised the mistake as soon as he received the papers and did immediately return all the documentation. However, the complainant, of course, had to be informed that someone else had received all their confidential information. Particularly in light of the fact that the complainant was already alleging a serious breach of confidentiality, this was another very serious error and led to the authority having to pay a sum of compensation in recompense.

    Use of a standard template clearly makes sense. However, this highlights the need, when setting up a system, of paying thorough attention to detail. Complaints often contain very personal information and every effort should be made to try and ensure that a complaint never accidentally falls into the wrong hands.

3. An important reason for sending the papers out in advance is to give the chair the opportunity to comment on the amount of time that it is proposed the panel should last.

    A chair was asked to chair a very complex complaint. When the request came in she was given just the one date. Not knowing the length of the papers and the number of complaints, she confirmed that she was available on that date. However, when she received the documents, which was luckily well in advance of the panel, she realised the complexity of the situation. The complaint in total ran to: the original complaint of 143 pages, the response to that, which ran to 110 pages, and the response to the current situation, which ran to 42 pages (and see further on this complaint in chapter 4). Fortunately the chair was relatively free from other commitments and she immediately indicated that there would have to be at least two days set aside for hearing the complaint. As it happened, the panel ended up lasting for three days (although not consecutive, the panel did manage to find three days very close together) and the panel took another whole day to make their findings and recommendations.

    The clear lesson to be learnt from this is that complaints managers should be alert to the possibility of overrun. If dealing with a very complex complaint, it would make sense to notify the intended chair well in advance and ask her for an opinion as to whether she wants extra time to be set aside in the event that everything cannot be dealt with in one day.

4. One chair in the research commented that when she first started sitting on panels she had problems with the information provided, as the following quotation shows:

I couldn't make head nor tail of it and, actually, looking back, it was a fairly modest set of papers. They can be difficult to follow. The papers start off in reverse order and then you get sort of a back flip to the complaint and this causes untold confusion. I usually use Post It stickers on them and I think the worst thing is when you don't know where something is and the complainant thinks you are a complete idiot and you have not got a clue what is going on. I bet any chair would differ as to how they would want the papers organised. I have noticed that the elected members immediately rip the whole thing up and change the order.

Careful thought needs to be given as to how papers are presented. If even chairs are having difficulty in following the order, it seems very likely that other attendees, including the complainant, will also have difficulty.

5. One respondent in the research illustrated the need for keeping the complainant informed as to the names and status of panel members, including where there has been a last minute change to the panel membership:

    It was my fault I didn't tell the complainant and when they arrived they saw the new panel member and said they were not staying with this person involved and that they knew her and she had had dealings with them in the past. We had to discuss whether to go ahead with two people and that was agreed. The complainant agreed but it wasn't ideal.

    Another respondent experienced a similar problem:

    We ask if they have any knowledge or anything which they object to about the panel members. We do not want a conflict of interest. In that case we would change the review panel. We had that once in respect of the panel member and once in respect of the advisor. The one involving the panel member was where the councillor had knowledge of the family and in fact had intervened with them in a number of situations; obviously you don't always connect a name without a face. It wasn't until the panel that the councillor declared that he had a previous involvement. On this occasion we had to adjourn to get someone else.

    An important issue arises from these examples, which is what should happen if one member of the panel needs to be disqualified? It costs a considerable sum of money to abandon a panel. Although it is not ideal, it is possible to continue with a panel with only two members, but this is only permissible if the complainant agrees. Care must be taken that this is a genuine agreement and that the complainant does not feel 'blackmailed' into continuing. If in doubt, the panel should be adjourned and reconvened at a later date with a fully independent panel. It goes without saying that every effort should be made to ensure that the original two members who were not disqualified are on the new panel. As confidential information is included about complainants, the less people who are privy to that confidential information the better.

6. When using a location for the first time it is not just non-authority premises that need checking for suitability as the following example shows:

    The social work department was situated upstairs in a building shared with other community providers. There was no way of entering other than via the reception downstairs. When the panel arrived the receptionist phoned through to the social work department, only to be told that no-one was expected. After some discussion, a member of staff from social work finally came down to speak to the panel. However, when she was told that members of the public would be attending the panel she point blank refused to let anyone enter the building. Eventually, after further lengthy discussion, a room was found in an adjacent building occupied by the probation service. However, this meant that no one could either enter or leave the building without a member of staff letting them in or out of a secure door, and this included gaining access to the toilets! Further, the room was full of old and broken computers, which all had to be moved into one corner in order for people to be able to sit round the table.

End notes

1. SI 2006 No 1738, reg 18(2).
2. *Getting the Best from Complaints*, para 3.14.2.
3. *Getting the Best from Complaints*, para 3.9.3.
4. *The Representations Procedure (Children) Regulations 1991*, SI 1991/894, reg 8(2).
5. SI 2006 1738, reg 19(4).
6. Unpublished paper sent to the authors by Dr Gillian Bridge, Dept of Social Policy, LSE.
7. The Commission for Local Administration in England *Report on an Investigation into Complaint No 99/A/5207 against London Borough of Hounslow* 29th March 2001, LGO: London.
8. In consequence the Local Government Ombudsman recommended a payment of £600 compensation.
9. The Commission for Local Administration in England *Report on an Investigation into Complaint No 01/C/07439 against Sheffield City Council* 20th June 2002 LGO:York.
10. Further discussion on who needs to attend the panel and why is contained in Chapter 4.
11. The Commission for Local Administration in England *Report on an Investigation into Complaint No 05/C/06420 against Sheffield City Council*, 2006/7 LGO:York.
12. (1999) 29 September (unreported).
13. I.e. the regulation requiring the panel to be set up within 28 days of the request for panel. Now reg 19(4).
14. [2000] 2 FLR 910.
15. The Commission for Local Administration in England *Report on an Investigation into Complaint No 02/C/08690 against Sheffield City Council* 9th August 2004 LGO:York.
16. At paras. 34 & 35.
17. SI 2006 No 1738, reg. 8(1)(a).
18. A complaint made outside the time limit may still be investigated where it would not be reasonable to expect the complainant to have complied with the limit and where, despite the lapse in time, the complaint can still be investigated effectively and fairly: SI 2006 No 1738, reg. 9(1)(2).
19. *Getting the Best from Complaints*, para 3.14.3. For the importance of making sure that the correct papers are sent out, see case study 2.

20. *Complaints Review Panels: A Good Practice Guide NCOG* (1998) Hamilton Training Service: Stoke on Trent, at para 3.2.
21. See Chapter 5 for a consideration of issues surrounding confidentiality.
22. *Getting the Best from Complaints*, para 3.14.3.
23. *Community Care Policy Guidance* Annex 1 Para 5 and the *Children Act Guidance* Vol.4 Para 5.44.
24. *The Commission for Local Administration in England Report on an Investigation into Complaint No 99/C/05229 against Shropshire County Council* 24th January 2002 LGO:York.
25. *The Commission for Local Administration in England Report on an Investigation into Complaint No 00/C/04141 against Lancashire County Council* 30th April 2001 LGO:York.
26. *Getting the Best from Complaints*, para 3.14.2.
27. *Children Act Guidance Volume 4*, para 5.46, and Community Care Policy Guidance Annex A paras 5 & 6; *Getting the Best from Complaints*, para 3.16.1.
28. *Complaints Review Panels – A Good Practice Guide* NCOG Hamilton Training Service: Stoke on Trent.
29. Consideration should also be given as to whether there are refreshments available, as a panel can be lengthy. There should be an area where all attendees can have a comfortable break.
30. *The Commission for Local Administration in England Report on an Investigation into Complaint No. 01/B/17272 against the London Borough of Bromley* 31 July 2003 LGO: Coventry.

Chapter 4

The Panel Hearing

This chapter looks at what happens when it comes to the actual day of the panel up to the point where the panel retire to make their recommendations: who should attend, pre-meetings and the hearing, and keeping a record of the panel.

Attendees at the hearing

The first issue is the requirement as to who should be in attendance on the day and what is their role at the panel.

The complainant

The most important person to attend the panel is the complainant, who has the right to attend panel.[1] It would seem reasonable to assume that the complainant, having requested the panel, would in almost all cases attend.[2] However, this assumption is not necessarily borne out and the complainant by no means always attends. It is not that infrequent that panels are convened and the complainant fails to attend. Provision should be made for the complainant to make a written statement if he notifies the complaints manager in advance that he will not be in attendance but wishes the panel to go ahead without him. However, best practice would dictate that the authority should do everything it can to have the complainant present at the panel. This is not necessarily easy to achieve. Getting the complainant to the panel may involve assisting him in finding someone to attend with him in an advocacy or support role, setting a convenient time and date and making the venue as non-threatening as possible.

Where the complainant fails to turn up to the panel either once, or on more than one occasion, with no prior warning, understandably the local authority may feel frustrated and will have to make a decision as to whether to proceed without him. If the complainant does fail to attend, one option is to try and contact him on the same day and make an offer to rearrange the panel. The complainant should be asked when he will be available. However, if the authority fail to get a response as to availability, it is a not unreasonable assumption that he no longer wishes to proceed. Sometimes the complainant might indicate that he may or may not attend. In these circumstances it will be reasonable to decide to continue without him, as rearranging a date will not necessarily mean he will turn up the next time.

It can be very difficult to decide to proceed without the complainant, even although an advocate has been sent in his place. If an advocate has been sent, the panel are entitled to assume that the advocate is fully informed and entitled to the information. But, where the advocate is a relative of the complainant, it may be that the relative might hear information about the complainant of which he was not aware and which is confidential or upsetting. Unfortunately the panel will not be in a position to know this. Consequently great caution needs to be exercised in such circumstances.

Complaints Panels in Social Care © Catherine Williams and Katy Ferris 2010 www.russellhouse.co.uk

Perhaps the most obvious situation where the complainant may not attend will be where he is in prison. Two principal options are then available to the complaints manager.[3] First, that the complainant can have someone attend for them or, secondly, that the complaints manager, either himself, or by delegating the job, go to visit the complainant and take a statement from him saying which areas of the report he is not satisfied with. This statement would then be supplied to the panel for consideration.

The chair has an important role to play where the complainant fails to attend but the panel proceeds. What should be attempted is to run it exactly as it would have been run had they turned up. The chair should try and get to the nub of the complainant's issues which are still outstanding after Stage 2 and ask questions that the complainant might have asked. It is not easy for chairs where the complainant does not attend. Their job is to be the neutral arbiter, not to represent someone. However, just because a party does not attend it should not mean that the department can simply put their case without being properly questioned.

The recent guidance makes provision for the non-attendance of the complainant. The guidance first of all makes it clear that it is absolutely acceptable for the panel to proceed in the complainant's absence but at his request.[4] Secondly, whilst the adult guidance stipulates: 'Should the complainant fail to attend a scheduled panel on more than one occasion, the panel should proceed without them',[5] the children's guidance is notably silent on this point. It is interesting to note the use of the words 'should proceed' in view of a general reluctance to do so in the absence of the complainant. This, of course, is guidance only and authorities may decide to make more effort than that given in the guidance in securing the complainant's attendance where the complainant is a child. Understandably an authority may be less tolerant of absence if the complainant is an adult.

A supporter to the complainant, including an advocate

Clearly one way of making sure complainants who are nervous, or who feel incapable of handling the complaint on their own, attend the panel is for them to bring a supporter on the day of the hearing. They are entitled to do this and they can be accompanied by any supporter, be it a relative or a friend [however, on this, see case example 1]. In addition they can have a person who acts as their representative and speak for them, including an advocate.[6] The regulations and guidance allow for any person who accompanies the complainant to speak on his behalf [see case example 2, for a rather unusual instance concerning an advocate, and case example 3, where there were multiple complainants].[7] It is considered good practice to notify the complainant of this right in advance of the panel hearing in order to allow the complainant to approach anyone should they wish to do so.[8] Complaints managers can assist complainants in finding a supporter to accompany them to the panel through advising them about help, for example from support groups or voluntary organisations.

In January 2004 the *Adoption and Children Act 2002*[9] amended the *Children Act* by inserting Section 26A. Under this section it is now a statutory right that children making complaints under the *Children Act* have access to independent advocacy or children's rights services. Amongst those who may well wish to bring a complaint are young people who were formerly in the care of the local authority but who left care aged 16 years, or who are now aged 18 years or over. By virtue of the *Children (Leaving Care) Act* 2000, which also amended the *Children Act*, these young people are also included in those who have the right to an advocate.[10] There is no similar statutory requirement to provide an advocate in the case of an adult complaining on behalf of a child. However, the guidance for adults provides: 'Some complainants may need advice and confidential support from an independent advocate to make their complaint, to pursue it, to understand the process and to cope with the outcome.'[11] The guidance goes on to say that the authority should consider how to meet complainants' needs, particularly those who are vulnerable.

An advocate may obviously play an important role in helping children to make their complaint and in supporting them through Stages 2 and 3.[12] Unfortunately the difficulty with the provision of an advocate is two-fold: authorities do not always have the budget for paying for an advocate and also they may not know beforehand the quality of the advocate who will be allocated to the complainant.

In relation to children, an advocate should be a person who is trained in supporting children and young people to have their voices heard. However, in the 2003 report of the Children's Rights director, children expressed their concern about the use and role of an advocate. The children responding felt that the best advocate might be someone that they knew and they had real reservations about involving a total stranger. An advocate was seen as someone to support and back the child in the procedure as well as a source of information to the child.

Local authorities who do not offer support in the form of an advocate to children may not only be in breach of their duties under the *Children Act* but they may also be held to be in breach of their duty under the *Human Rights Act 1998* and Article 8 of the *European Convention on Human Rights*.[13] It is becoming increasingly recognised that children have the right to be involved in decision-making. Case law on this is developing in the direction of the child being represented in any decision-making and this would obviously be achieved by the involvement of an advocate.[14]

In some instances the complainant may wish to bring an individual who is legally qualified. This is considered below.

Children attending a panel

The research showed that not many children actually attend a panel hearing. However, if a child is going to attend it is important to bear this in mind. Very careful consideration needs to be given to the preparation for the panel, right down to small details such as careful seating arrangements. The key factor is the need to ensure that children are comfortable and that they feel confident that they will be listened to and enabled to say what they need to say. It is vitally important that they are not intimidated by the procedure [see case example 4].

There are a variety of reasons why children may not attend a panel, which include factors such as age and competence. However, one possible explanation for the low number of children making it to panels is the length of time that the process as a whole can take. In total it is normally over three months. Children usually complain about issues which are in need of being resolved as soon as possible, so Stage 1 is much more helpful to them and complaints are liable to be resolved at this stage. Furthermore, where a child does proceed to Stage 2, the authority may go that bit further to achieve a resolution, rather than allowing the case to proceed further to panel.

Legal support

For the complainant

Where he wants a supporter the complainant should be encouraged to bring one with him to the panel. This view is supported by the guidance. However, where the supporter is found to have legal training, then some authorities may become very uncomfortable with the idea. The worry can be that it is turning the panel into a quasi-legal hearing.

The original guidance[15] specifically stated that a complainant could bring a supporter who was legally qualified, but that the supporter must be made aware that they were not there acting in a legal capacity, but purely as a supporter. This approach is echoed in the new guidance for adults, where it stipulates that if bringing a supporter to speak on their behalf, 'this person should not be a barrister or solicitor acting in a professional capacity.'[16] However, the children's guidance does not mention a legally qualified supporter, presumably on the basis that if a child is bringing someone with him to speak for him, it will be the advocate who has assisted him at Stages 1 and 2.

Many authorities have not had any experience of a lawyer attending in support of the complainant. However, there are equally many authorities that have experienced a lawyer coming to provide support. Where the complainant has advised that his supporter is a lawyer, the complaints manager must then inform the complainant that the lawyer is not to be paid for his time by the local authority and that he will be there in a non-legal capacity has largely been a very positive experience and to be welcomed. Lawyers are said to have kept things moving when the complainant has got stuck on an issue. They are also thought to be very focused, concentrating on the real and crucial issues, not getting sidetracked on to minor details. They have been clear on what it was they wanted to express and spoken in clear terms. They have taken some of the inevitable emotion out of the proceedings, which is helpful. Lawyers seem to understand that the process is not an adversarial system and that they are there to listen to what is being said and to respond. This practical experience is in marked contrast to the comment and advice in the guidance that no one should feel the need to be represented by a lawyer and that 'the presence of lawyers can work against the spirit of openness and problem solving'.[17]

It would seem that lawyers can play an important role in keeping things on track during the panel and can be of benefit to all those present. Further, if the practice is followed, that where complainants notify the complaints managers that they are bringing a legal advisor, the complaints managers then has discussions with their own legal advisors about the complaint and the issues arising, this should mean that everyone understands the issues and is well prepared for the day.

The issue of the use of a legal advisor at a panel arose for consideration in the High Court in *R (on the application of LP) v. Barnet London Borough Council.*[18] The parents of a young man with multiple disabilities had attended a panel with a pupil barrister and a representative from their solicitors. At the outset they made an application to be legally represented by the pupil barrister and for the representative to be allowed to remain to take a note of the proceedings. This application was opposed by the local authority, who said it would be unfair, as the authority had no legal representation. Also, they were worried that the note-maker could misrepresent them and were concerned about the use that the parents might make of the notes. The panel took the decision it would be necessary to adjourn the hearing if legal representatives were to be allowed. The parents were unwilling to agree to an adjournment and therefore agreed to continue without legal representation, having been told that the lawyer could wait outside and that they were free to seek her advice at any time. The parents were also told that they could not have a note-taker. An experienced note-taker was provided to the panel and a copy of his notes would be provided to them.

On an application for judicial review challenging these decisions, the parents relied on the decision in *R v. Leicester City Justices, ex parte Barrow*,[19] which concerned the question of whether an unrepresented defendant had the right to the assistance of a friend in the magistrates' court. Mr Justice Dyson easily distinguished the parents' case. He said:

> *I readily accept that the issue here is one of fairness. What fairness demands in a court of law where a defendant is facing a criminal charge will not necessarily be the same as what fairness requires in the informal atmosphere of a panel meeting convened pursuant to the regulations that apply in these cases. The fact that the panel convenes 'meetings' rather than conducts 'hearings' is, I think, revealing of the difference. I do not accept the submission of Mr Wise that there is a presumption of law that an unrepresented party is entitled to legal representation in informal meetings, such as those convened by panels under these regulations.*[20]

He similarly dismissed the argument that the case should be likened to one involving solicitor representation at a child protection conference, where, in another case, the Council had an absolute policy not to allow such representation.[21] Here it had not been contended that a panel had such an absolute policy of never allowing legal representation. Dyson J went on that this was a most unusual case where there was a background of recriminations and previous legal proceedings by the parents. An adjournment would not have taken very long and the panel was placed in a difficult position. They had offered the parents a choice. Either to adjourn to allow the Council representatives time to obtain legal representation, or to proceed without legal assistance, but with their legal representative available should they require her. The panel had acted reasonably and lawfully.

With regard to the note-taker, Dyson J thought there was no real prejudice to the parents in not being allowed to have their own note-taker. There was an experienced note-taker present and the panel had resolved the matter by deciding that his notes would be supplied to the parents as soon as the meeting was concluded. This had happened and it was not suggested that the notes were in any way incorrect or incomplete in material respects. The suggestion that the refusal to allow the parents' note-taker to remain in order to take a note as being unlawful was 'quite fanciful'. The panel had exercised their discretion on this issue in a fair and sensible way. It followed that he rejected both the challenges to the decision of the panel.

As a corollary to this decision, it is not common practice for the local authority to have a legal advisor with them at a panel. Clearly, where a local authority legal advisor attends, then good practice would be to allow complainants to have their own advisor. It would be contrary to the rules of natural justice for the local authority to have a legal advisor but for the complainant to be refused a lawyer. Therefore, where the authority does wish to bring legal assistance, the complainant should be informed of this. However, what is not clear is whether the authority should assist the complainant at all in having their own legal support at the panel. If the authority feel the need to have their own legal advisor, it would suggest that the complaint has a legal issue of substance to be argued. Consequently, good practice would suggest that in such circumstances the authority should, at the very least, put the complainant in touch with a suitable firm of solicitors. Furthermore, it is also suggested that, should the complainant so request, assistance should be given to the complainant in meeting any reasonable costs incurred as a result of using a lawyer.

Legal advisor for the panel

In the recent guidance reference is made to the fact that various principles should be observed in the conduct of panels, including that panels should observe the requirements of the *Human Rights Act 1998*, the *Data Protection Act 1998* and other relevant rights-based legislation and conventions, in the discharge of their duties and responsibilities; and that the standard of proof applied by panels should be the civil standard of 'balance of probabilities' and not the criminal standard of 'beyond all reasonable doubt'.[22] These are quite clearly expected legal requirements of the panel, which, if the panel members are neither lawyers nor had any training on the running of panels, may not necessarily be easy to observe, particularly in complex complaints and those where the interpretation of statute, regulations, guidance and policies are at issue. In such a case, a legal advisor may be very necessary to assist the panel [see case example 5, which details a very complex complaint].

The view of the Local Government Ombudsman is that provided the complainant is aware that the legal person is there to advise the panel, to clarify the law to them, then that is perfectly satisfactory. However, any legal person should not be volunteering and contributing to the panel. The Local Government Ombudsman has come across complaints where it would appear that the legal advisor has basically answered everything that has come up, as if he were in court, even though that is not his position. This is highly unsatisfactory. The Ombudsman is of the view that some local authorities have taken the approach that a complaint gives rise to an adversarial situation. This is wrong. The panel is not akin to a court hearing and it is wrong to give complainants that sort of impression.

As a general rule of thumb, if the papers have been properly read in advance, the chair should be able to assess whether there are legal questions that need dealing with. The chair should then contact the complaints office, pointing out that some legal answers are needed and please could they be supplied. In this way provided the chair gets it right before the day, this should limit the number of times a legal advisor might be needed.

The good sense in having a legal advisor present in difficult cases can be demonstrated by a report by the Local Government Ombudsman[23] in which an organiser from a learning difficulties support group complained that the panel were not *au fait* with the legal issues relevant to the consideration of the case. He went on to give the example of the chair asking an irrelevant question. The local authority argued that it would not be reasonable to expect all members of a panel to be completely in command of all the relevant legislation but that they had legal advisors present and legal officers and they had quickly stepped in to explain that what the chair was asking was an irrelevant consideration. Despite this, the Local Government Ombudsman report recommended that a payment of £500 be paid to the complainants in recognition of the delay, stress and anxiety they had been caused.

An issue that does need addressing is how to actually secure legal advice for the panel, as it must be the case that the same person cannot both advise the staff and the panel. The reason for this is that clearly there is the potential for a conflict of interest and, as a general rule, having the same advisor for both staff and panel gives rise to the potential for such a conflict. A way round this difficulty and suggested good practice for such a situation is to have a system whereby if legal advice is sought it should be from a person within the local authority, but not someone connected with social services. Thus the authority can then operate under a Chinese wall system, only using advisors to panel who have nothing to do with complaints.

Other personnel

The original practice guidance[24] stated that 'the members of the panel will need to have access to the appropriate personnel.' The current guidance states that 'panels should be conducted in the presence of all the relevant parties'[25] and goes on to list those who should be in attendance at the panel.[26] Other than those attendees considered above, there are a number people who should, or might, be invited to attend the panel. Careful consideration needs to be given as to who should be in attendance, as it is important to ensure that the purpose of the panel is achieved wherever possible. This is likely to be done not only when all relevant parties are present, but also when the panel is conducted in the right atmosphere. The Local Government Ombudsman does have some concerns about whom individual authorities are choosing to have in attendance at the panel. The issue of how many people attend has given them cause for concern, as well as the danger of it turning into a mock court room drama.

Complaints manager

As the person who is responsible for managing the complaints process, it is essential to the panel to have the complaints manager present for any queries they may have about the process. The complaints manager is not there to be a supporter to the complainant, but neither is he there as part of the social care department. The complaints manager has a difficult role, as he is paid by the local authority and must answer for the work of the complaints unit, but other than that he must attend panel purely in an advisory role, not attempting to influence the outcome in any way.[27]

In a Local Government Ombudsman Report, concern was expressed that the complaints manager had attended the panel in order to present the local authority's case alongside the officer.[28] Furthermore in that particular authority the complaints manager himself investigated Stage 2 complaints. Unfortunately this is not as unusual as might be hoped. The issue of concern is that the complaints manager is there to make sure the correct procedures are followed. The Local Government Ombudsman may find maladministration if they are not. The complaints manager is not at the panel to represent the local authority, to put forward their side. It is totally inappropriate for the complaints manager to have any role other than facilitator on the day of the panel.

Investigator

When a complaint is investigated at Stage 2 the guidance requires that:

> *The complaints manager should ensure that the authority appoints an investigating officer (IO) to lead the investigation of the complaint and prepare a written report for adjudication by a senior manager. The IO may be employed by the local authority or be brought in from outside the authority, appointed specifically for this piece of work. The IO should not, however, be in direct line management of the service or person about whom the complaint is being made.*[29]

Obviously this person needs to attend the panel.[30] The very fact that the complainant has gone to panel means that the panel members may wish to seek clarification as to the contents of the investigation report and the way in which the investigation was conducted, for example why a particular individual was or was not interviewed. As the investigator will have reached conclusions on the complaint, the panel will also need to be sure that these conclusions have been reached correctly. Furthermore, it is possible the panel may wish to overturn some of the investigator's conclusions. The Local Government Ombudsman would undoubtedly expect the investigator to be present. The absence of the investigator might certainly lead the Local Government Ombudsman to question whether or not it allowed the panel to have a balanced view. They would be looking at what was explored and whether the panel was incapacitated by the absence of the investigator.

The guidance does allow for a panel to go ahead without the investigator. It provides that should the unavailability of the investigator lead to inordinate delay in holding the panel, the chair should take a view on proceeding without him present.[31] However, there are real dangers in doing this. The unfortunate outcome might well be that the complaints manager might get drawn in to an inappropriate role of answering for the investigator. Realistically, unless the investigator is either unwilling or unable to attend for a very considerable period of time, to attempt to go ahead with a panel without the investigator would be foolhardy. In the event that a complaints manager is faced with such a difficult dilemma, perhaps the best solution would be to try and obtain the original investigator's notes of interviews and copies of relevant papers, if at all possible, and to ask another investigator to thoroughly familiarise himself with the case and attend the panel in the original investigator's stead. Alternatively, it may be that, depending on experience, the independent person might be able to take the place of the investigator.

Independent person

The *Children Act 1989*, section 26(4) specifically requires that at least one person who is not a member or officer of the local authority takes part in the consideration of a complaint and any discussion about action to be taken. Additionally, the regulations provide that an independent person must be appointed.[32] This will be a different person from the investigating officer, regardless of whether the investigating officer is an internal or external appointment. The independent person works alongside the investigating officer.

The experience of *Voice for the Child in Care*, an organisation which supplies independent persons, is that in most cases where they have supplied an independent person, an invitation to attend panel has been made where they have been involved at Stage 2. As the regulations require an independent person to be involved in all considerations for resolving the complaint and the panel shall consider 'any oral or written submissions which the independent person appointed in accordance with regulation 17(2) wishes to make'[33] it would be incorrect not to invite the independent person to panel.

In common with the investigating officer it is possible to go ahead with a panel without the independent person if they are unavailable for a long time. Unlike attempting to go ahead without the investigator, it may be more acceptable to go ahead with a panel where the independent person cannot attend. This is because the independent person has a particular role, which is to make sure that a proper investigation is carried out. It is not the independent person's job to do the actual investigation. Thus, although it is not possible to know what questions will be raised by the panel, and the independent person may be able to help with any questions, generally speaking independent persons have little to say other than reinforcing what the investigating officer has said. However, if the independent person has put in a report which is either critical of the way the investigation was undertaken, or disputes any of the investigating officer's findings, then it would be vital to ensure that the independent person also attended the panel.

Adjudicating officer

A complaint is, and should always be regarded as, one against the department and not individual members of staff. After completion of the investigation at Stage 2 it is the role of the adjudicating officer to consider the complaint, findings, conclusions and recommendations of the investigator and independent person. The guidance provides that the adjudicating officer should normally be a senior manager who reports to the director. A senior manager means a manager in the authority with a sufficiently senior position to make strategic decisions regarding service delivery.[34] It is up to the adjudicating officer to provide a response to the complaint, including a decision on each individual complaint and whether or not the authority agrees with the Stage 2 findings and recommendations. It is also the role of the adjudicating officer to ensure that any recommendations contained in the response are implemented.[35] If the adjudicating officer has rejected any of the investigator's findings at Stage 2 he should attend the panel as the authority's representative, but where he has accepted them all it will usually be acceptable for him to delegate the responsibility.[36]

The presence of the adjudicating officer, or his representative, at the panel is clearly necessary, so that the department is represented. The panel members may wish to ask the adjudicating officer how any decisions relating to the complainant and the complaint were taken. He should be able to deal with any such questions or queries whether raised by the panel or by the complainant. The panel may also wish to ask more general questions, for example, about the organisation and delivery of the service which is the subject of the complaint before them.

Once any recommendations from the panel have been approved, it is normally the responsibility of the adjudicating officer to implement any actions which are recommended to resolve the complaint and to implement any changes in service delivery which are recommended as a result of the findings and for which they are responsible. So it makes sense, both from a practical point of view and as part of the learning curve from listening to complaints, to have the appropriate manager present to hear the particular issues in full.

Independent sector providers

If there are any independent sector providers involved in the complaint, it may be that they will have already dealt with their own part of the complaint under their own complaints procedure. However, regardless of whether or not this has already happened, thought should always be given as to whether or not it would be appropriate to invite them. Particularly where the work of the department and the independent sector provider are closely intertwined, and where the complaint intertwines the two, it may make good sense to at least invite them.

Witnesses and experts in the field

There can be a degree of confusion as to whether individuals should be called to play the role of 'witness' to the panel. As the purpose of the panel is neither to re-investigate the complaint nor act as a court of law, this should generally be thought neither appropriate nor necessary. Further, as a report is submitted after the Stage 2 investigation, any individuals who have some particular knowledge to add to the complaint should, at least in theory, already have been spoken to. Furthermore, if witnesses are called, the panel will be in danger of descending into becoming a complaint against an individual rather than the department, which is not appropriate.

However, although witnesses of fact are generally not appropriate, it may be possible to consider people who might be able to offer a professional opinion about a particular aspect of the complaint. Then it might be appropriate to ask an expert witness or advisor to attend. An example of where a panel might wish to do so would be one that involved breach of confidentiality. For that, it may be relevant to have someone such as a personnel manager present to advise the panel.

There is a clear argument for limiting the number of people who are at a panel. The guidance does make provision for the attendance of what can be termed an expert witness by stipulating that the chair should make the final decision as to who should be in attendance, including asking the authority to make specific members of staff available to provide specialist advice or opinion.[37] However, ideally, if the investigation has been thorough at Stage 2 the panel should not require witnesses or experts to attend. Provided the papers are sent out in time, that is at least 10 days prior to the panel, then the chair should have the opportunity to arrange for any further required information to be supplied. If this cannot be arranged, only then should the presence of a particular person be needed.

A clerk to the panel

The usual practice is for either the complaints manager or a secretary or administrative member of staff, who has been responsible for making the arrangements, to take on the role of clerk. The guidance states that 'anyone providing administrative support should also attend' and that 'the authority will need to provide administrative support for the operation of the panel which may be in the form of a clerk. It may be sensible for this role to be filled by a separate officer to that of the complaints manager.'[38] Limiting the number of people present at the panel makes sense. Having more people than is necessary may create a more intimidating atmosphere for the complainant and it may also involve the authority in unnecessary expense. Particularly where the panel hearings are recorded, the complaints manager should normally provide ample administrative support, leaving the decision whether or not to have a clerk up to the discretion of the authority. The authority, rightly, may not want to provide a clerk except in exceptional cases. This appears the most sensible option.

Pre-panel meeting

Many authorities have a meeting of the panel members prior to the hearing and in some the complaints manager and/or the clerk or legal advisor, if there is one, is also present. However, some authorities have decided to move away from this practice and others have always taken the view that such a meeting is inappropriate. There are reasons for dismissing a pre-panel meeting as part of the procedure. There is a fear that the panel might form a view prior to commencement, which would clearly be unacceptable, and a worry that complainants could think they had not been able to put their side forward before there was any discussion, tainting the process.

However, those authorities that do have a pre-panel meeting take an entirely different, diametrically opposite, approach when considering the role and purpose of the meeting. The view is that the meeting can ensure that people do *not* make up their minds in advance.[39] In addition, it can be used as an important opportunity to deal with any additional information or to seek it out if it is thought to be missing. So, if issues are puzzling the panel members, or if the complaints manager has any last minute information, this can be brought up. Also, if there are any extra papers that have been submitted post the panel papers being sent out, it gives the panel the opportunity to discover what this late submission is about, why it is late and check that it is suitable to accept. It can also give the complaints manager the opportunity to give the panel a bit more information about the history of the complaint, which could be very complex. The information given on paper may be only a percentage of the full story and setting the complaint in context can assist the panel in getting a clearer understanding of the problem.

The guidance makes it clear that having a pre-panel meeting is entirely acceptable. Reference is made to a pre-panel meeting, describing it as an opportunity for panellists to meet in closed session to discuss the order of the business and any other relevant issues, such as taking legal advice.[40] Thus, the guidance does not specifically advise either for or against such a meeting. Whether or not a pre-panel meeting is good practice is not an entirely straightforward issue. From the perspective of a suspicious complainant, it could be seen as a time when the complaints manager and panel can have discussions about him and be swayed into a decision before they have met the complainant, reinforcing any 'them and us' perception he may hold. On the other hand it can be a valuable opportunity for the chair or complaints manager to establish that the other members have read and understood the papers and may even allow them to head-off any preconceived bias. So, good practice would be to reinforce to the complainant that the pre-panel meeting is not the start of the main decision-making but merely a chance to clarify issues before the start. This would probably best be done by making it clear in the information sent out to all attendees that the meeting would be taking place and what its purpose is [see case example 6 for the importance of ensuring that any pre-panel meeting is properly planned as part of the day].

The procedure for the hearing

Once all the parties required are in the room, a basic procedure for who speaks when is necessary. The guidance sets out a basic procedure to be followed, which conforms closely to what was found to be happening in practice in the research.[41] The following could be considered as the 'standard' procedure which operates in practice:

- The chair of the panel will introduce herself and then either ask everyone present to introduce themselves or personally go around the room identifying all the people there.

- The chair of the panel will open the meeting, explain its purpose and then go on to outline the procedure to be followed.

- At this point it is usual to remind everyone of the need for confidentiality.

- The chair invites the complainant (or their representative) to give a summary of their complaints and the reasons for their dissatisfaction with the decision/s made at Stage 2 of the complaints procedure. Many authorities will not limit discussion in any way here and will allow both the complainant and their supporter/representative to speak.

- The chair will ask any questions and then invite the other members of the panel to ask questions of the complainant/representative to clarify anything they have said or to query anything with reference to the panel papers submitted.

- The chair will then invite the manager from the service to outline the department's decision/s relating to the complaint and the reasons for them.

- The chair will then allow the panel members to ask the manager any questions they wish to have answered or any points they want clarification on.

- The investigator will be asked if he wishes to contribute anything or he may be asked during the discussion to clarify a point. This will be the same where the independent person is present.

- The chair will then ask the complainant and anyone attending in his support if they wish to add anything and to sum up his complaint, ensuring that the complainant has the last say in the main section.

- The chair or the complaints manager will then make the complainant aware that the panel will withdraw to make their deliberations and that he will be notified of the outcome.

The guidance also comments that: 'The chair should also indicate how long the panellists anticipate that the presentations should last' and that 'the purpose of hearing the presentations is to understand each party's opinion of the complaint rather than an opportunity to cross-examine attendees'.[42] The former point may sound good in principle, but in practice how long a panel is anticipated to take will not necessarily bear any close relationship to how long it actually lasts. On paper it may look as if a panel will either be very short or very long, but it can be surprising how wrong such an estimate can be.[43] The latter point is an interesting one of principle. Particularly where things appear to have gone badly wrong, this is an opportunity for the complainant, and the panel, to question the department closely. The difference between 'questioning' and 'cross-examining' is not necessarily very obvious.

It is clear from the structure both in practice and in the guidance that the chair plays an extremely important role on the day. However, whilst providing a written structure to the chair as to how things should be run, it will not necessarily happen exactly in the given format and what happens on the day is likely to vary. Also, some chairs will have a slightly different way of doing things. This does not matter, as, provided the fundamental basis of the panel is followed, that is everyone is given the opportunity both to have their say and to ask the questions they wish to ask, following an exact pattern is not necessary. Also, while it is all very well having guidelines, sometimes the meeting does not go as planned. Consequently the chair has to respond to that [see case example 7]. Further, the more complex the complaint and the more issues for consideration, the less likely it will be that things will go according to plan.

The duration of the panel

There is no set guidance on how long the panel should run for. The research found that an 'average' panel will take about half a day. The issue for duration is that the complainant should feel that they have had the opportunity to say anything relevant which they wish to say and that the panel has the chance to query anything arising from the papers or having any matter which is unclear clarified.[44]

As a general aim it clearly makes sense to aim to finish a panel in one day, although very occasionally the panel will spill over into a second day where it is a very long and complex complaint.[45] There is a real concern that should the panel last for more than a day, then the function of the review panel will be in question, with the panel in danger of getting too far into investigating the complaint, rather than reviewing what has led to the panel. Additionally, panel members all have different commitments and so understandably attempts must be made to draw the meeting to a close within one day with time for the panel to make their deliberations.

The Local Government Ombudsman's view on duration is that it is likely that the office would uphold a complaint if the complainant was not allowed to say what he wanted to say [see case example 8 for an example of where the LGO is likely to find against an authority]. However, with the consent of the Local Government Ombudsman, it would be possible to limit the time given to a complaint without it leading to a successful appeal. An example of this arose where the complainant had initially raised over 50 complaints and had submitted a huge amount of paperwork to the investigator to consider. Subsequently the complainant went to panel. In the meantime the complainant bombarded the complaints unit with paperwork, such that there were over 800 documents sent in which the complainant wanted the panel to consider. This was clearly impossible. In light of this the complaints manager, in agreement with the panel chair, contacted the Local Government Ombudsman to ask whether it would be permissible to limit the amount of time available to the complainant. The Local Government Ombudsman agreed to this. The arrangement was reached that, provided the complainant and the department were both given an equal amount of time in which to present their case it would be fair to limit the hearing in this way.[46]

A record of the meeting

The local authority is under no specific duty to take minutes of the main panel hearing, although in *R v. London Borough of Lambeth, ex parte Al-Azawi*[47] it was considered to be a matter of best practice. The National Complaints Officers Group also sensibly believe that minutes provide further assistance to the panel members when making their recommendations. Furthermore, if the complaint goes to the Local Government Ombudsman, minutes may be useful, not just where the complainant remains dissatisfied with how his complaint has been dealt with, but also where the complainant raises concerns about the panel itself. As one of the duties of the clerk to the panel, the guidance provides that the clerk should 'take notes to facilitate the panellists decision'.[48] This is not quite the same as suggesting that there should be minutes of the meeting, although it is clearly a sensible suggestion. The provision of a note-taker clerk is in line with the recommendation of the National Complaints Officers Group that a note-taker should receive a copy of all the papers and that such a person should attend and fulfil no other role whilst at the hearing.[49] The National Complaints Officers Group guide also recommends that the members of the panel should agree the wording of the notes and that the panel chair should then sign these, which could then accompany the recommendations. All this could also simply be done by the complaints manager.

There are a number of different ways of keeping a record of the panel discussion. Some authorities simply have a record in the form of brief, written notes, usually taken by the complaints manager; some have a recording of the panel; some have a typist in the room who types the minutes of the panel; and some have a minute taker. Whatever method is used, some sort of record should be taken and anything is better than nothing.

The view of the Local Government Ombudsman office is that recording the panel is of the most assistance and is increasingly likely to continue to be so. As pointed out, someone may take a complaint to the Local Government Ombudsman and include in their grievance that the panel did not listen to something. Listening to a recording can demonstrate whether or not this allegation can be substantiated. In one of the reports issued by the Local Government Ombudsman one of the complaints was that:

> He had not been given the opportunity to say at the review panel what he had wanted to say and to ask why some issues had not been addressed.[50]

However this authority did minute the panel meeting and the notes taken by the clerk at the panel showed this allegation was not true, and that in fact the complainant had raised many issues and had asked several questions.

Another Report into an investigation said that Southwark local authority had been at fault for not telling the complainant that they would not agree to his request to tape the panel.[51] The complainant in this instance was deaf and although he was bringing a supporter he wanted the panel recording. The Report does not say whether the recording should have happened, but does take the view that the complainant should have been informed of the refusal to do so prior to the day and found the authority at fault.

Key points summary

- The expectation should be that the complainant will normally attend the panel.

- If the complainant fails to attend, attempts should be made to reconvene the panel with the complainant in attendance.

- A supporter or advocate can speak for the complainant.

- Children have a statutory right to an advocate in the complaints process.

- If a child is attending the panel careful thought should be given to the arrangements to ensure the child is comfortable and feels able to contribute.

- If a complainant brings a lawyer to the panel, the lawyer is not there in his professional capacity.

- If the authority wish to have a lawyer assisting it at the panel, it should inform the complainant and should assist the complainant in finding a lawyer himself, if he so desires.

- Any legal advisor to the panel should not also give advice to the department.

- The complaints manager should attend the panel in an administrative capacity only.

- The investigating officer should be expected to attend the panel. The panel should only go ahead without him in very compelling circumstances.

- The independent person should attend the panel, although where the independent person is in total agreement with the investigating officer it may be appropriate to go ahead without him if he is unable to attend.

- The adjudicating officer attends the panel as representative for the department and to provide a response to the complaint.

- It may be appropriate to invite an independent sector service provider if the provider has also been complained about.

- It is not appropriate for witnesses of fact to attend the panel other than in exceptional circumstances.

- If it is necessary, it is preferable to obtain expert advice prior to panel, rather than have an expert attend.

- A clerk to the panel should be present solely in an administrative capacity.

Complaints Panels in Social Care © Catherine Williams and Katy Ferris 2010 www.russellhouse.co.uk

- Any pre-panel meeting should be confined to discussing the business of the day and the issues which the panel might wish to raise.

- The panel chair should set out clearly the procedure for the day at the start of the hearing.

- The panel should last for as long as is necessary to deal with the complaint. An arbitrary time limit should not be put upon the proceedings.

- The meeting should be recorded in some format. An audio recording is preferable.

Practice illustrations and case examples

1. There can be dangers in complainants asking relatives to attend, as is shown by this quotation:

   We had a case where the advocate turned up and said the complainant had not felt able to attend. So we began with the advocate, who was a relative of the complainant. He then heard some upsetting things about the complainant and then said he felt he could not represent her and so we had to reconvene. Then neither the complainant nor the advocate attended and we didn't hear anything else from them. So that was a bad experience.

   The lesson that needs to be learnt from this example is for complaints managers and chairs to be very aware of the nature of the complaint before them. If, contained within the papers, are allegations which, if borne out, expose information of a very sensitive nature and the complainant indicates that he intends bringing a relative with him to panel, it would be wise to check with the complainant that he does fully appreciate that the allegations will have to be tested. The complainant should be informed that this will inevitably involve discussing private information and that he therefore needs to consider carefully if he would prefer to keep it confidential.

2. It makes sense that only those people who are complainants are entitled to an advocate. Thus, although other people may be involved in the complaint, the panel must confine itself solely to a consideration of the aspects of the complaint which relate to the particular complainant. The following example shows how this can give rise to the question as to whether or not someone is complaining:

   A co-complainant turned up to the panel with an advocate. However, he then said he was not actually a complainant and he did not intend staying, but that he wanted his advocate to stay. The panel told him if he was not a complainant he could not have an advocate. Therefore, if he wanted his advocate to stay, he had to agree that he was a complainant. After consulting with the advocate he declared that he agreed that he was a complainant and left the meeting. The panel considered all the complaints, including his views on the complaints as put forward by the advocate, which were not always in accord with the other complainant's views. In their findings and recommendations the panel included their decision regarding the advocate. The complainant then went on to complain to the Local Government Ombudsman that he was forced into agreeing to be a complainant. The Local Government Ombuds-man supported the panel's approach.

3. It is clearly possible that there may be a group of people who wish to complain. For example, if a decision is taken to close a children's home the children, parents and carers may have views on this decision. If such a complaint arises there needs to be careful planning in advance:

> *There were 12 complainants, all of whom were parents or carers of service users, with a set of several complaints. All of them had agreed that this represented their complaint. The panel met with all 12 complainants present. A whole day was set aside for the meeting, which was in a neutral venue. All three panel members were external independent people, living outside the authority. The ground rules had been worked out in advance through discussion and agreement with the complaints manager. One complainant acted as the spokesperson and addressed each complaint. Each complainant then had the opportunity to make comments through their spokesperson. The investigating officer and the department could then comment on each complaint. When the panel asked questions sometimes one parent answered through or on behalf of the spokesperson. Each complainant was invited subsequently to make any further comments specific to their own experience. All the parties went away happy that this format worked well.*

Such an approach will only work if the nub of the complaint is agreed between the various parties. Where the parties have different views, it would not be possible to combine them all into one hearing as each case would need to be listened to separately to see if the complaint for the particular individual was borne out.

4. The importance of proper preparation by the complaints manager prior to a panel is demonstrated by the following example of a case where a child was attending:

> *We had a child come to panel. It was very much a case of thinking about how to prepare around their needs, with careful consideration. It is about what is best for the child. We try to keep it informal. We thought carefully about seating arrangements. They, of course, had an advocate. We gave them the opportunity to speak with the panel face-to-face, on the understanding that the panel would have to share with the others what was said. It is about allowing the child to feel confident that they are listened to and that they can say what they need to. You need to take away the intimidation factor from the procedure. The balance becomes even more important when you are dealing with the child complainant.*

5. When it is important for the panel to take legal advice and how lawyers should behave is well illustrated by the following case example, which raised three different important issues:

The chair of the panel is a lawyer

When the complainant sent in his first record of complaint it ran to 143 pages. This was not just information about his actual complaints, but contained in the papers were copies of guidance, parts of legal judgments and so on. Added on to the end of his first volume, however, which detailed a long history of his dissatisfaction with how social care were dealing with him, his ex-partner and his child, the complainant also raised current problems concerning the monitoring of arrangements for contact with his daughter, which he said were in breach of a recent court order. This led the investigator to produce two reports. One dealt with the historical complaints, which is what the investigator had originally been given, and one dealt with his current complaints which were of some urgency, as the complainant was complaining that the lack of attention to them meant he was not having contact and his daughter was being alienated from him. This meant that at the panel there were three bundles of papers. The original complaint of 143 pages; the independent investigator's findings on the original complaint which ran to 110 pages; and the findings on the current situation which ran to 42 pages.

As it happens, the person who was going to chair the complaint was a lawyer, so she was perfectly capable of dealing with the legal issues in the complaint. However, the issue here is whether or not a chair should do so in such circumstances. There are three points to make on this. First, in a case where legal material is quoted, it is not just, as here, the sheer length of the papers, but also the selection of legal materials, which requires consideration – is it correctly quoted, taken out of context and so on? It is suggested that it is not the job of a panel chair to sift through and make judgments in this way, as she might then be appearing to be acting as a lawyer for one side or another rather than being neutral. Secondly, where court proceedings have taken place, a chair must be very conscious of the fact that the panel must not in any way make any findings or recommendations which interfere with the proper court process. Lastly if, as happened here and is almost inevitable in such a complex dispute, the department plans on sending legal advisors to the panel, there is a clear need for the panel to be legally advised.

Panels are not courts of law

It is crucial that any lawyer who is attending panel, regardless of which party they are advising, does so understanding this basic point.

In this complex dispute, not unreasonably, the department decided that they should send a legal representative to the panel. However, they sent not one but two legal personnel. It then became evident that one of the legal representatives was going to try and point score against the complainant. At every opportunity that he could, when the complainant spoke, he would interrupt and say 'on a point of order' you can't do this, say this, hear this, or whatever. Despite the chair reminding the lawyer, on a number of occasions, that this was not a court of law governed by strict rules of evidence and of court procedure, he persisted. Eventually the chair asked the lawyer what he actually thought he was doing at the panel, why he had come. His response to this was that he did not know!

The question for the chair is: what should she do? It is perhaps fortunate in this case that there were two lawyers present. This made the decision relatively easy and straightforward and is what happened – the offending lawyer was asked to leave. However, even where there is just the one lawyer, the decision should still be the same and the lawyer asked to leave if he will not comply with the chair's instructions. It is always possible for a departmental lawyer to be available on the end of the telephone and lawyers must not be allowed to hijack the proceedings.

Court rules concerning contact with the parties do not apply

As above, lawyers must understand this basic point.

> *Subsequently the other member of the legal team complained about the panel. He sent a letter to the complaints manager on the third day of the hearing, complaining that during the refreshment breaks the panel were having private and unrecorded discussions with the complainant. He then threatened himself to withdraw from the panel unless matters were tightened up.*

This raises a different point for the chair. Here the lawyer was not disrupting proceedings, but had gone through the correct channels to make his objection known. However, he did not appreciate that during breaks at a panel it is perfectly acceptable, and indeed polite, to talk to the complainant, provided the panel confines itself to matters other than the complaint. If it is important that the department have a legal representative present, if possible, due to the nature of the dispute, it is not then helpful to ask a lawyer to leave if he does not appreciate the nature of the proceedings. The better way of dealing with it is to speak to him in private and explain how complaints panels operate, which is what happened here.

6. Where authorities do have a pre-panel meeting, it is important to consider if they have the space set aside for such a meeting:

> *We had one panel where I asked the complainant to arrive 15 minutes early but they arrived earlier than that and I had to ask the complainant and the Director to leave and I actually arrived last anyway which was even worse. It meant that the briefing I had with the panel was very brief and we were conscious of the other people milling around.*

This quotation shows that it is important for different times to be given to the various people attending the panel. Generally it is suggested that it would be wise to give the panel 30 minutes for the pre-panel meeting. It does not matter if the panel have too much time before the panel commences but it does matter if they have too little.

7. It is not just complainants but other people present who may require the chair to respond to them sensitively in order for the panel to run smoothly, as is shown by the following example:

> *I think it is very important for the chair to be in control, obviously, because you have to rein people in. Also the complainants can be nervous etc. so if you are going to get through the panel with success you must keep control of what is going on during the course of the day. Although you might allow the complainant a bit of rope initially, because it is their day in court and they want to have their say, you allow*

them a bit of leeway, but once you have got into things you mustn't let things stray off the point and get too personal or start looking at complaints that have not been investigated. I had one complaint where the complainant brought an elderly neighbour as his support. This lady obviously felt very strongly that the authority had victimised him and was desperate to say so. It was clear that she would not sit back until she had had her opportunity to speak. So I actually started by going to her. She then stood up and declaimed for about 10 minutes. Once that was over and she was satisfied she had been listened to she sat back quietly and did not take any further part in the proceedings.

8. One of the complaints managers in the research had strong views on not allowing the panel to run on:

   I am very keen on three hours for panel and that seems long enough. I think people should be able to say what they need to in three hours so I wouldn't agree to half-day panels or something like that. It starts at 6 p.m. and finishes at 9 p.m.

This example demonstrates a totally inappropriate attitude towards the complaints process. Other than in extreme circumstances it is not for the complaints manager to decide how long a panel should last; that is not the underpinning philosophy of the process. The idea is that the complaint is that of the complainant and it is that person's right to have enough time set aside for a proper and thorough examination of the complaint.

End notes

1. *Getting the Best from Complaints*, para 3.15.1.
2. In some circumstances the complainant may be acting on behalf of a service user who has died.
3. Although see Chapter 3, in which it was suggested that it may be possible for the complaints manager to organise that the panel actually be held in the prison.
4. *Getting the Best from Complaints*, para 3.15.2.
5. At 3.17.5.
6. See below on legal support. The origin of this stipulation is in the provision of a 'McKenzie friend', who is allowed to appear in court to represent an applicant. The roots of the McKenzie friend is found in a divorce case, *McKenzie v. McKenzie* [1970] 3 All ER 1034. In court the instruction to judges is that while the final decision rests with them on whether to allow a McKenzie Friend, the presumption will be in favour. It is seen as helpful to the administration of justice for party litigants to perform as well as they can in the intimidating environment of a courtroom.
7. See originally the *Children and Young Persons Representations Procedure (Children) Regulations 1991* (SI 894), para 8(6) and the *Children Act Guidance Volume 4* para 5.45. Now see SI 1738, para 19(6). See case example 2, for a rather unusual instance concerning an advocate, and case example 3, where there were multiple complainants.
8. National Complaints Officers Group (1998) *Complaints Review Panels: A Good Practice Guide*. Stoke, Hamilton Training Service.

9. S. 119.
10. For the various qualifying conditions see the *Children Act 1989* ss. 23A, 23C and sch. 2, para 19B.
11. *Learning from Complaints*, para 3.4.2.
12. The role of the advocate was originally established under the *Advocacy Services Representations Procedure (Children)(Amendment) Regulations 2004*, SI 719. Guidance is also provided in *Get it Sorted: Providing Effective Advocacy Services for Children and Young People making a Complaint under the Children Act 1989* DfES 2004.
13. Art. 8(1) provides: Everyone has the right to respect for his private life, his home and his correspondence.
14. See *Claire F v. Secretary of State for the Home Department* [2004] 2 FLR 517 where it was held that if the decision to separate a mother and baby was to be Article 8 compliant, then the Secretary of State's obligation was to ensure that the baby was properly represented.
15. *Complaints Procedures Community Care in the Next Decade and Beyond 1990 Policy Guidance* Ch.6, Annex A section 5.
16. *Learning from Complaints*, para 3.17.1.
17. *Getting the Best from Complaints*, para 3.10.3.
18. (2000) WL 1791622.
19. [1991] 2 QB 260.
20. At 46.
21. See *R v. Cornwall County Council, ex parte H* [2000] 1 FLR 236.
22. *Getting the Best from Complaints*, para 3.11.2.
23. The Commission for Local Administration in England *Report on an Investigation into Complaint No 99/C/02624 against Gateshead Metropolitan Borough Council* 28th February 2001 LGO: York at para 81 & 82.
24. *The Right to Complain: Practice Guidance on Complaints Procedures in Social Services Departments* DoH & SSI London: HMSO 1991, at para 4.17.
25. *Getting the Best from Complaints*, para 3.11.2.
26. ibid at 3.15.
27. Some complaints managers take on the role of recording what happens at the panel. For consideration of this see below.
28. The Commission for Local Administration in England *Report on an Investigation into Complaint No 99/C/02624 against Gateshead Metropolitan Borough Council* 28th February 2001 York: LGO.
29. *Getting the Best from Complaints*, para 3.6.4.
30. ibid at para 3.15.2.
31. ibid at para 3.15.2.
32. SI 1738, reg. 17(2).
33. ibid reg. 19(5)(b).
34. *Getting the Best from Complaints*, Annex 1.
35. ibid, paras 3.8.
36. ibid, paras 3.15.3.
37. ibid, at para 3.15.4.
38. ibid. at para 3.15.5 and Annex 1.

39. See on this, Chapter 2, case example 2.
40. *Getting the Best from Complaints*, at para 3.16.3. The guidance makes it clear that no deliberations on the complaint should commence at this meeting.
41. ibid at paras 3.16.4–3.16.7.
42. ibid at para 3.16.5.
43. See further below.
44. See case example 3 in Chapter 3 for the importance of allotting the necessary amount of time for a panel.
45. And, probably uniquely, one of the authors has chaired a panel which lasted for three days and then deliberations took a fourth day.
46. The complainant did, then, amongst a variety of issues that he took to the LGO, challenge the amount of time he was given at panel. However, his complaint on this matter was not upheld.
47. (1998) 11th June, Unreported.
48. *Getting the Best from Complaints*, Annex 1.
49. National Complaints Officers Group (1998) *Complaints Review Panels: A Good Practice Guide* Stoke: Hamilton Training Service.
50. The Commission for Local Administration in England *Report on an Investigation into Complaint No. 99/B/3078 against Kent County Council* 6th March 2001 LGO: Coventry at para 86.
51. The Commission for Local Administration in England *Report on an Investigation into Complaint No 99/A/00988 against the London Borough of Southwark* 12th March 2001 LGO: London.

Chapter 5

Recommendations of the Panel

At the end of the open panel hearing the chair of the panel will bring the main meeting to a close and will retire with the other members to consider their findings and recommendations.

   This chapter considers: what happens in order for the panel to come to their conclusions; the types of recommendations which may be made; time limits for making the recommendations; who is involved at the recommendation stage and confidentiality. In addition the situation where a panel are not in agreement is considered.

Panel deliberations

When deliberating it is important that the panel draw conclusions based upon the evidence which they have seen and heard at the panel hearing. In order to assist them the panel should make sure that they see any notes taken of the meeting which will assist them. These notes may have been taken by the complaints manager and/or any note-taker. In addition, chairs should make notes themselves about the main points and preferably so should wing members. Where the panel are satisfied that the department has, in fact, behaved appropriately and correctly based on the events and evidence presented, it is permissible for the panel simply to state or declare they have no comments to make in relation either to specific individual complaints or to the whole complaint. However, best practice dictates that some explanation, albeit brief, should be given as to how they have reached this conclusion.

   Unlike the Local Government Ombudsman, the panel does not have to establish maladministration to uphold a complaint. They merely have to find that the complainant has a justifiable cause for complaint in order to make such a finding and consequent on that they may or may not choose to make a recommendation. When making any recommendations the panel need to consider two elements: firstly, what the complainant is seeking and secondly, the most appropriate redress for the situation.

Time pressure

Originally the *Social Services Inspectorate Direction 8*[1] and the *Children Act Regulations 9(1)*[2] required a panel to decide on its recommendations within 24 hours of the hearing. In light of this it is not surprising that it has been normal for panels to make their recommendations straight after the main hearing. However, whilst this may generally be an appropriate and sensible time frame, there are problems in some cases with it being so rapid. Thus, whilst it is important that the findings and recommendations are made swiftly, one problem which can arise is where there has been a long session and people are inevitably winding down and cannot concentrate properly. On top of this there may also be the extra pressure in that the panel may need to vacate the premises where they are meeting. Haste under these circumstances can mean that the need to weigh up the material in light of all the evidence is not done as carefully as it should be. Furthermore, if there is not sufficient time for the panel to conclude its business, but the members cannot physically meet the following day, it may be that some members cannot check what is hastily sent round via e-mail. All of these factors could additionally have the knock-on effect that the recommendations are then unclear and it is difficult to understand the reasoning; or indeed the reasoning may not be evident at all in the final report containing the recommendations. Experience has shown that many complaints managers have regularly chased the panel chair by phone or email to check that the recommendations were agreed upon, as, although they had been drafted on the day by the clerk or complaints manager, they needed to be confirmed as accurate as soon as possible the following day.

Probably in recognition of the difficulties that the 24-hour time limit imposed, the new regulations now allow longer for panel deliberations. The new limit is five working days.[3] This is to be welcomed from the point of view of haste. However, in some, maybe nearly all, instances it is still likely that the panel will be unable to meet physically within the new timescale. Therefore, although it relieves the time pressure to rush out the panel findings, particular care still needs to be exercised to ensure that all the findings and recommendations are agreed and couched in clear terms.

Personnel present during the closed session

Practice varies from local authority to local authority as to who is present during the panel closed session. Normal practice for many has been for the complaints manager to be present. Some authorities have not had a general practice, but have decided depending on what the panel want at that stage, and some have taken the decision that the complaints manager should not be present. Those who have said that the complaints manager should not be present consider it inappropriate for him to be there for reasons of perceived independence.

The disparity of approaches on this point is attributable to the previous lack of guidance clarifying who should or should not be present. This has now been addressed, to a certain extent, under the new guidance, although the guidance is not worded in exactly the same way for both procedures. The children's procedure is somewhat vague, as it states: 'The panel may need administrative support' but this should not unduly influence the panel's deliberations and no conflict of interest should arise.[4]

There are two ways of looking at this issue. On the one hand there is an argument that, in a situation where complainants are increasingly concerned about independence, the complaints manager, who is employed by the local authority, should not be in the private deliberation session. However, on the other hand and as discussed later, the need to have the complaints manager present can arise from the chair wishing to have the complaints manager act as clerk for the panel and in doing so write down the recommendations. Further, in many authorities it is clearly believed that it is helpful to have the complaints manager present, so that he can answer any questions the panel may have about the possible ramifications of the recommendations that may be considered. The same can equally be said about a clerk or note-taker. Depending on the level of knowledge and seniority of such a person the clerk/note-taker may be valuable in assisting the panel to come to workable recommendations. Contrary to that, of course, such a person could attempt to influence the recommendations, which was certainly the experience of one chair in the research undertaken by one of the authors. Ultimately, both sets of guidance highlight that whoever is present that person should not unduly influence the panel's deliberations.

Confidentiality and storage of panel papers

The previous guidance was more explicit than the current guidance on the issue of confidentiality. It recommended that all the members of a panel be bound by the normal practices of confidentiality in terms of all that they see, hear and read on the day of the panel and prior to that.[5] Also, the *Policy Guidance*[6] and *Children's Guidance*[7] required the authority to draw the issue of confidentiality to the attention of the independent people. In the third Overview Report of the social services Inspectorate the recommendation was made that the independent persons sign an undertaking of confidentiality[8] and their Standard 13 required all those involved to have due regard for confidentiality. Finally, also in the third Overview Report,[9] the social services Inspectorate recommended that all papers be returned to the department at the close of the panel.

The current guidance refers to confidentiality by providing that the investigating officer should have access to all relevant records, which should be released within normal confidentiality bounds;[10] if the media is involved, to maintain strict confidentiality;[11] with regard to the administration of the panel, that local authorities should confirm confidentiality protocols;[12] and that the chair should commence the hearing by explaining the need for confidentiality.[13]

The recommendation that all papers be returned to the department at the close of the panel is the item of particular relevance here. This recommendation has been endorsed by the Local Government Ombudsman's office, which considers that the panel papers should always be handed back to the department to be shredded. The research found that all local authorities were aware of the need to collect the papers in after the panel. However, unfortunately they do not necessarily always achieve this.[14] Authorities need to keep a copy on file and dispose of all the extra sets distributed to panel members and staff, but some find that as people disperse quickly they sometimes go away taking their papers with them. On this subject the Local Government Ombudsman caution that should a panel member take the papers away and the papers then get out into the public, or fall into the wrong hands, or be misused, that the expectation would be that the Local Government Ombudsman would uphold a complaint.

However, the requirement to return all papers at the end of the panel is not as straightforward as first appears. There is an obvious difficulty with a very commonplace situation, where the chair wishes to keep the papers until she has confirmed the recommendations.[15] Furthermore, there is an issue of even more pressing difficulty. It can be argued that whilst all other attendees should return their papers, it would not be practical for the chair to return them, as they need to be kept for three years to cover the possible reference of the complaint to the Local Government Ombudsman or to cover any other legal action taken by the complainant. This is a highly pertinent point, which departments need to address. The compromise solution suggested is that the complaints manager should store the papers on behalf of the chair. Alternatively, if the decision is that the chair should keep the papers, this should be agreed on the basis that the chair should always bear in mind the issue of confidentiality of storage and ensure that the documents are properly destroyed after a certain agreed period of time, three years being the usual limitation period.

Majority or unanimous verdicts?

The *Community Care Policy Guidance*[16] previously stated that if a panel member disagreed with the majority recommendation, this view, and the reason for it, should be included in the panel recommendations, and the more recent guidance has a similar provision.[17] Perhaps surprisingly, in the research undertaken there were only a handful of authorities that had not always had a totally unanimous[18] decision.

Unanimous decisions can be put down to a variety of reasons. For example, it could be due to how well the parties state their arguments, the basic merits of the case or it could be down to the wing members being happy to be led by the chair. However, with the increased numbers of independent persons sitting on panels, it may be that there will be an increase in the number of dissenting opinions. Whether or not this proves to be the case, the panel should still make their recommendations in line with the majority, but where there is dissent that needs to be clearly recorded.[19]

A common theme found in the research when talking about the recommendations stage was time pressure to make the recommendations and leave. It was clear that this meant that the wing members were willing to go along with the chair's view, if it meant that they could get away more quickly. Therefore a unanimous verdict was being achieved due to time pressure and not necessarily through the thorough discussions of the panel. Further, unfortunately some seemed surprised at the suggestion that it is permissible to have any disagreement amongst the panel and for many it appeared that they would rather remain until a unanimous decision was made. Clearly this is of concern, as it may mean that it simply comes down either to who has the time to stay or who can be the most obdurately persuasive of the three panel members. Quite apart from the guidance positively stipulating that it is permissible, there is no real reason why a dissent should not be accepted and recorded[20] and the decision left to the director to consider. Should the director agree with the minority view, he would then need to give a strong reason for doing so. Particularly where the chair is in the majority, the majority viewpoint should normally sensibly be followed. The reasoning for this is that the chair is the person who ought to have led the questioning and who was appointed both for her independence and for her ability to make reasoned decisions. The chair should have read and studied the papers at length, knowing that it is her duty to be taking a stronger lead than that of the wing members. However, it is worth noting that now the panel is made up of three independents,[21] this is arguably a slightly different case, although the chair will still often be the individual who has the most expertise in chairing meetings.

Types of recommendations

Generally the remedies which are available to the panel are not fettered by legislation or regulations which stipulate permitted remedies. This in itself is bound to give rise to a variance in the way local authorities deal with resolving complaints after the panel meeting. However, what is universal is that the panel is not allowed to recommend that any disciplinary action be taken against individual members of staff. Staff are always entitled to statutory protection as the authority must go through appropriate procedures before they can discipline a member of staff.[22] It is commonplace in complaints for an angry complainant going to panel hoping to have an employee's 'head on a plate'. The complaints manager, and chair where appropriate, need to make it clear to complainants that this is not a possible outcome.

As has happened in practice, in some hearings the members of the panel may only feel that they should make a general recommendation to the director for him to take some action (of his choosing) in relation to certain aspects of a complaint. They therefore make the recommendation that action should be taken, but leave it open to the director to choose the type of action he feels appropriate. However, it is suggested that this is not good practice. It really should be for the panel to make clear recommendations, which the director then has to consider and either accept or reject [and see case example 1 for a case demonstrating how important it is for the panel to tease out exactly what it is the complainant is really complaining about]. This is certainly the view of the Local Government Ombudsman, who believes that any failure to make specific recommendations is something that needs to be tackled in the guidance. From the perspective of the Local Government Ombudsman, it does not make sense that a complainant has gone through the process and then has to come to the Ombudsman because no specific remedy is offered by the panel.

The research established that the Local Government Ombudsman's office had found that many chairs of panels shy away from making recommendations, believing that it is not their role. This finding was based upon the training sessions that the Local Government Ombudsman's office had been involved in over the years and from their investigators speaking with chairs during an Ombudsman investigation. The Ombudsman's office considers that panels are actually in a better position to make recommendations than their office is, because panels can simply consider the merits of a professional decision, even though there has not been maladministration. This, of course, gives panels a much wider remit than the Ombudsman.[23]

Whilst there are remedies available to panels ranging from an apology to financial reimbursement, it was clear from interviews with chairs of panels, as well as some of the complaints managers, that some panels are not aware of the power that they wield. They should, of course, have been made aware of this in the panel papers or have received appropriate training at the time of appointment. However, it is also worth bearing in mind that where a financial remedy has been offered by the local authority this will normally have resolved the complaint and such a complaint is much less likely to progress to Local Government Ombudsman level, including those cases where the remedy offered is not as much as it could be or as much as the complainant wanted.

In a presentation to the National Complaints Officers Group, given by Pat Riley, an Assistant director of the York Local Government Ombudsman office,[24] she commented that the Local Government Ombudsman have expressed concern in the past at the failure of panels to consider remedies other than an apology, (although this is not something which appears to have been highlighted in the Local Government Ombudsman Annual Reports). She also pointed out that case law has established that panels can criticise the merits of a professional decision irrespective of whether or not there has been maladministration. When it came to the issue of the Local Government Ombudsman finding examples of avoidable fault in managing complaints, the list included: failure by panels to fulfil their role in a sufficiently robust and independent way;[25] failure by panels to consider the issue of remedy; failure to hold the panel within a reasonable time frame; and failure to understand the powers available to them.

Financial reimbursement and/or compensation

A prominent issue for panels is that of compensation. Up until 2000 there was a great deal of confusion as to whether local authorities and panels had the power to make an award of compensation to a complainant. However, the *Local Government Act 2000*, Section 92(1) made it clear that panels do have the ability to award compensation. The section states:

> *Where a relevant authority consider:*
> (a) *that action taken by or on behalf of the authority in the exercise of their functions amounts to, or may amount to, maladministration, and*
> (b) *that a person has been, or may have been, adversely affected by that action, the authority may, if they think appropriate, make a payment to, or provide some other benefit for, that person.*

Each local authority has the discretion to decide whether the panel can make monetary awards. Particularly following the introduction of the *Human Rights Act 1998* and a society that increasingly encourages claimants to bring claims in tort, local authorities cannot ignore the provisions of section 92.

Chapter 6 of the new guidance gives helpful examples of the types of situations where financial redress may be sought and the types of remedies which may be awarded. Thus in paragraph 6.1.1 it states:

> *There are different reasons why financial redress may arise. These include:*
> * *compensation;*
> * *quantifiable loss;*
> * *loss of a non-monetary benefit;*
> * *loss of value;*
> * *lost opportunity;*
> * *distress; and*
> * *time and trouble.*

And in paragraph 6.1.2 this is followed up:

> *When considering financial redress, the local authority should also consider the following issues:*
> * *whether it is appropriate to offset compensation in instances where the complain-ant owes money to the authority. This would apply for any costs owed to the authority as a whole, rather than to a single service;*

- *where the complainant has incurred expenses or suffered financial loss, the authority should also consider whether it is appropriate to pay for loss of interest as well. The Local Government Ombudsman recommends the standard rate set by the County Court; and*

- *it may also be appropriate to calculate a financial remedy as a formula which takes into account all known factors.*

What is clear, therefore, is that what must be separated out when dealing with the question of payments is whether the panel are awarding recompense for loss or awarding compensation. If the former, in many cases it is relatively straightforward that what the complainant is asking for is a reimbursement of calculable losses. If this is so, then it is simply a matter of the panel doing a calculation of the amount and awarding that sum. [See case example 2 for an example of a difficult decision for the panel to make when considering reimbursement of a complainant's legal fees.] However, not all cases are as straightforward by any means.

However, in other cases the remedy cannot be such a straightforward monetary calculation. If a decision has been taken that is found to have been incorrect and there have been financially non-quantifiable consequences, such as fractured relationships, distress or anxiety, then no amount of money can repair the emotional damage. This then gives rise to the difficult issue of, first, whether the panel should make an award and, secondly, if it should, the amount of any award. Not surprisingly, some local authorities are very reluctant to allow their panels to make monetary recommendations, instead they are happy to let the issue go to the Ombudsman, who then suggests an amount. However, some local authorities have found that the Local Government Ombudsman office has not always been happy with such an approach, not liking such an open-ended recommendation. Those authorities that do allow panels to make a monetary recommendation very rarely permit them to put an actual figure on the amount, they merely state that the director should consider the issue of recompense [see case example 3 for an example of an authority which does allow its panels to recommend not just awards but also to put a figure on the amount of the award].

It is arguable that some panels are being required to make monetary recommendations which are beyond their capabilities. This was the view of one Local Government Ombudsman office who said: 'It sounds simple, but a lot of panel members are not happy with making payments and have no real experience. They are often assumed to have this experience when it is not necessarily the case at all. They make some really poor decisions, because they are not properly supported or supervised in actually doing the job.'

The research found that the perception amongst a majority of local authorities was that it was not only prior to the *Local Government Act 2000* that the panel could not make any recommendations on financial payments at all, many had not realised that compensation could be awarded even after the passing of the Act. This is not surprising given that some of the complaints managers were not aware of the ability to make such recommendations. Furthermore, the Local Government Ombudsman also took a cautious view of what panels could recommend prior to the passing of the Act. In one Local Government Ombudsman Report, involving the London Borough of Bexley,[26] there was an allegation that the complainant had been discouraged from pursuing her complaint to a panel on the grounds that the panel could not recommend financial compensation. The Local Government Ombudsman report said:

Review panels have no express power to make recommendations for the payment of financial compensation. At the time of the events I have investigated, some councils were of the opinion that they had no general power to pay compensation for administrative faults. The main elements of the complaint had been upheld by Stage 2. I do not consider that it was unreasonable therefore for the local authority to tell the complainant that it thought she would have nothing to gain by taking her complaint to a panel and to advise her to consult a solicitor if she wishes to seek financial redress.

Nowadays a fairly commonplace and sensible way of dealing with the issue of compensation is to pass the question on. Thus, if the panel considers someone might be entitled to compensation the case will to go straight on to the insurers or to a payments panel. It is suggested that this is a helpful way of coping with the problem. The trouble with relying on panels is that they do not normally have either training or expertise in this area, as pointed out above by the Local Government Ombudsman.

It is clear from the research that understandably local authorities are in general extremely uncomfortable with the issue of awarding sums of money at panel. If we return to the consideration of the variety of people who sit on panels, it highlights the difficulties surrounding this issue. Not only would it be difficult to imagine that local authorities, which have very differently constituted panels, would be making the same awards, but even within authorities it would seem likely that, without extensive training, different panels would reach differing amounts. There is also the concern that whilst there are people sitting on panels who were formerly elected members, or who have formerly worked for social services, some of them will be very concerned with the pressures on the finances of the local authority and be unwilling to make monetary awards.

Amongst the reasons why authorities have been so reluctant to make monetary recommendations in the past is the fear that by so doing the authority is admitting fault and thereby laying itself open to legal action. However, the *Compensation Act 2006*, section 2, makes clear that an apology in itself does not amount to an admission of negligence or breach of statutory duty and, similarly, the payment of money, either as reimbursement or in compensation for errors or poor practice, by no means necessarily amounts to an admission of legal liability for breach.[27]

In *Anurfrijeva and Another v. London Borough of Southwark*[28] the Court of Appeal considered the approach to be adopted by the courts when considering claims for damages under the *Human Rights Act 1998*. The court followed the earlier decision of Mr Justice Sullivan in *Bernard v. LB Enfield*[29] that, in deciding the quantum for damages where human rights are breached by the maladministration of a public body, the recommendations of the Local Government Ombudsman can be looked to for guidance on the appropriate compensation. The Court of Appeal stated that complainants should generally turn to the Local Government Ombudsman, rather than the courts, where they are claiming damages as a result of maladministration. The Court of Appeal also stated that the Local Government Ombudsman has the advantage that the office can award comparable amounts to the courts and offer a service which is free and does not involve lawyers in all instances. The speed of resolution for the complainant was also highlighted as being better than that of going to court.

In their *Annual Report* of 2003/2004[30] the Local Government Ombudsman welcomed this approach by the court saying:

> Jointly with the Parliamentary and Health Service Ombudsman we have written to the Lord Chief Justice about some of the issues it raises. Not least among these is the time constraint on bringing an action in the High Court: three months is unlikely to be sufficient for us to decide a complaint in time for a complainant still to seek permission for judicial review. On the other hand once complainants take court action the law is clear that they cannot have a 'second bite' by bringing a complaint about the same issue to the Ombudsman.

Also as a result the Local Government Ombudsman revised their guidance on remedies. They published a guide on remedies in 2005.[31] In dealing with financial compensation they list the typical situation where it may be relevant: cases involving delay causing injustice; where no practical action can provide an appropriate remedy; where the complainant has suffered financial loss; and where he has suffered distress and anxiety. The report then goes on to distinguish between quantifiable loss and loss of a non-monetary benefit. In relation to the latter the report, at paragraph 22 says:

> Quantifying the loss of such benefits can be extremely difficult. The starting point should be to identify:
>
> - what the presenting needs of the complainant, or the person on whose behalf a complaint is being made, were at the point when some fault occurred;
>
> - what practical provision should have been made or what service, support or provision should have been in place to meet those needs, and how frequently;
>
> - what the delays or failures in making the provision or gaps in services and support were, over an identified period of time; and
>
> - what the consequences were for the complainant and/or the complainant's family or carer of the failures: specifically, in the absence of the provision, service or support which should have been supplied, how were the assessed needs met, if at all, and by whom.

This guidance is available to local authorities, who can then decide how to implement the guidance within the authority [see case example 4 for a doubtful suggestion as to one form of financial redress].

Other remedies

Compensation is only one option that is potentially available to panels. They can also make a variety of other types of recommendations:[32]

- an explanation and apology to the complainant [see case example 5 for an illustration of how not to apologise]

- require the local authority to provide a service

- suggest a change of service/re-assessment of need

- ask for a review of procedures on a specific issue

- arrange staff training

- review a particular policy in light of the issues raised in the complaint

- recommend the local authority meet appropriate timescales to avoid unnecessary delay

- recommend the authority monitor the effectiveness of the remedy.[33]

Although, of course, disciplinary action is not also a remedy that can be sought at panel as one chair in the research pointed out: 'We can make quite powerful recommendations from an individual's point of view. Obviously we cannot recommend discipline, but having said that the panel can recommend that the department should look into the practice of someone to see if it should then mount disciplinary proceedings. That is quite a powerful recommendation from an individual's point of view so I think we have extensive powers.' [See case example 6 for further comment on recommendations.]

The most important thing is for the panel, when making its decision, actually to come to conclusions as to what might then be done to rectify the situation. In the *Local Government Ombudsman Annual Report 1998/99* one of the local government ombudsmen drew attention to three aspects of the operation of the statutory social services complaints system, including that:

> *Some review panels had not adequately analysed what harm the complaints had suffered as a result of fault and recommended an appropriate remedy.*[34]

In the same report the Local Government Ombudsman expressed a hope that central government would include advice about this in revised guidance on social services complaints. This is taken up in the new guidance, where it is stated: 'Attempts at resolution should not end once a complaint has been made. Rather, there should be continued efforts to resolve the dissatisfaction of children and young people so that the matter complained about is resolved during consideration of the complaint.'[35]

A record of the outcome

Whatever the panel decides they must record the reasons for their findings and recommendations in writing[36] so that when the director considers the recommendations he is clear as to the reasoning and outcome the panel have decided upon. This requirement has gained extra significance since the introduction of Article 6, that a fair hearing presumes that a reasoned judgement will be given,[37] and in a Local Government Ombudsman report the Ombudsman encouraged panels to word their reports in a clear and, if need be, forceful manner.[38]

It is not unusual for an authority to have a system whereby the chair is not the individual who actually writes the recommendations. So whilst the chair will lead and coordinate the discussion and deliberations it will be the clerk or the complaints manager who writes the recommendations. These recommendations are then seen by all the members of the panel who approve them. Whilst there is no reason why this should not happen, a note of caution needs to be entered if this is the system in place. A complainant might not consider this appropriate, as he has gone to the panel to present his argument to an independent panel. From his perspective, as the local authority is the employer of the clerk or complaints manager then he may feel that if the panel chair is not the person writing the recommendations the panel is not independent. However, the other side of that argument is that although chairs are not straightforward employees of the authority, they still get paid to sit on panels. In that sense they are similarly not entirely independent.

In light of the fact that chairs are paid for their role and are normally taken from professional backgrounds, it must be hoped they have the skills to write the recommendations.[39] Certainly writing recommendations should be a feature of any training where it is the chair who does write them. In one Local Government Ombudsman Report it was considered that the 'written decision of the panel was plainly inadequately expressed and inadequately reasoned. No explanation was given of what the Council's irregularities and shortcomings might be. These faults in the way in which the panel communicated its decision were maladministration.'[40] The Ombudsman went on to recommend that a review of training be undertaken to include the panel members. This serves to reinforce that the recommendations require careful thought and presentation on the part of the panel.

Where it is the complaints manager or clerk who writes the recommendations, then clearly they must be sent to at least the chair of the panel for her full approval. It is further suggested that they should also be sent to the wing members. This gives all members of the panel the opportunity to alter anything they disagree with or wish to have worded differently [see case example 7 for an instance when the complaints manager was inappropriately involved in writing the recommendations of the panel].

Informing the complainant of the outcome

The recommendations of the panel and reasons for them need to be made in writing to:

- the complainant

- the local authority

- the independent investigator

- the independent person

- and anyone else with sufficient interest.

The normal practice at the end of the panel hearing is to ask the complainant to leave, having explained that the recommendations will be sent to him, with an estimate of when that will be. In a minority of local authorities the panel chair will ask if the complainant would like to wait. However, this latter practice is not recommended. It can put pressure on the panel to hurry in their deliberations or can result in the complainant waiting perhaps a number of hours for the findings to be reported to him. If the authority prefers to give the complainant a quick resumé of the outcome then a telephone call by the complaints manager later in the day, or the following day, resolves this desire.

Key points summary

- The panel do not have to find maladministration to uphold a complaint. They merely have to find the complainant has justifiable grounds to complain.

- The panel has five working days in which to draw up their findings and recommendations.

- It is entirely acceptable for the complaints manager to be present during the panel deliberations, although only in an administrative and support capacity.

- Panel proceedings are confidential.

- Panel papers should be returned to the authority to be shredded.

- The chair may wish to hold on to her papers, in case of further reference to the Local Government Ombudsman or legal proceedings. She should have a safe storage system and a confidential method of disposing of the papers after three years.

- The panel can reach a majority verdict. Any dissenting opinion should be recorded.

- The panel have the ability to award both financial reimbursement and compensation.

- Payments panels, or a reference to the authority's insurers, for calculating an award of compensation is the better option, due to possible inconsistencies in approach if left to individual panels.

- Panels have a wide variety of other remedies available to them, of which they should be aware.

- The panel must record the outcome of their findings and recommendations.

- It is acceptable for the complaints manager or clerk to write down the findings and recommendations, but the chair must approve them before they are sent to the director.

- The panel recommendations must be made known to the complainant, the authority, the investigating officer and the independent person.

Practice illustrations and case examples

1. Sometimes the complainant will not get to the nub of the complaint when wording his complaint. It is important for the panel to bear this in mind when making findings and recommendations and for the panel to ensure that they tackle the root problem. The following case illustrates this point:

   The complainants were parents of a severely disabled child. At the panel it became clear that the department appeared to have a blanket policy, with no discretion at all, surrounding matters of lifting and handling. This is illegal and was therefore subject to a recommendation by the panel. However, in addition the panel considered that one of the complaints raised had not been properly investigated. The actual complaint was that 'our views and wishes have been consistently ignored'. This is a rather wishy-washy nebulous complaint which it is difficult to get a grip on and the investigator had not upheld the complaint. However, in considering this particular complaint it became clear, and it was admitted by the department that, despite the parents' requests, no care plan or core assessment had been done due to departmental incompetence. Therefore the panel, whilst not upholding the complaint as such, could make a finding and recommendations surrounding the failure, which was not the subject of a specific complaint but did show that the parents' views and wishes had been ignored.

The lesson from this is for panels to be alert to teasing out what it is that complainant is really talking about and being ready on the day to deal with it. If the panel finds malpractice during the course of the hearing they should not ignore it but should take steps to remedy it.

2. It will not normally be the case that legal costs incurred by the complainant will be recoverable. In light of the fact that the complaints system is meant to be readily accessible to all and is not supposed to require legal assistance, it is the complainant's choice to go to a solicitor. He will therefore have to bear the cost of that choice. However, it is not always that straightforward, as the following illustration shows:

The case revolved around possible deprivation of assets. The investigator had concluded that although the actual complaints were largely not made out, there had been a fundamental flaw in the department's decision-making. The case had proceeded throughout on the basis that the complainant's mother had deprived herself of an asset, her home, in order to avoid payment of care fees. But, what should have been in the department's mind was whether or not it should use its discretion to disregard the property, as the complainant perfectly fitted the guidance description of when an authority should so disregard, as she had given up her own home in order to go and live with, and care for, her mother. The investigator therefore recommended that the case should be looked at again in order for the department to decide how it wished to exercise its discretion. This view was accepted by the department and it would therefore be a reasonable assumption that such a case would not go to panel. However, what then became an issue was the fact that from fairly early on the complainant had employed a solicitor. She had done so, as she was in very serious danger of losing her home.

The difficult point here was what should the panel do, faced with some quite considerable legal costs? On the one hand you could say that all these costs were reasonably incurred by the complainant, in view of the department getting things wrong, and she should therefore be reimbursed all her money. On the other hand, you could say that as she had a solicitor from an early stage that it was up to the solicitor to get the law right. He should have advised her properly and the extra costs she incurred were due to his failure to challenge the department robustly early on. Therefore, if she had any grounds for complaint about her legal fees she should take it up with her solicitor. It was not the authority's responsibility. Ultimately the panel decided that as the solicitor had correctly pointed out the disregard provisions from early on, but the department consistently treated the case as one of deprivation throughout, the complainant should be reimbursed her full legal costs. This was even though the solicitor, after correctly pointing out the department's error, had in effect gone along with the department and argued the complainant's case on the basis of deprivation rather than disregard.

The learning point from this case surrounds the use of lawyers in general. Although for the most part it is not up to the local authority to pay legal fees, which also cannot normally be paid for under legal aid, as with all decision-making bodies a panel must be careful to give consideration to a request for legal fees and not fetter its discretion by refusing all such requests. In the case of *R v. East Sussex County Council, ex parte W,*[41] in proceedings for judicial review, counsel for a boy had pointed out that there is no provision for legal aid in complaints and it is unlikely that a child could afford legal representation. The judge in that case simply acknowledged the point and then went on to say that in ordinary circumstances the complaints procedure would provide a suitable alternative remedy.

3. In one local authority in the research, the panel were permitted to make monetary awards, including specifying the amount of the award. The complaints manager made the following comment:

   We had a case recently where we didn't expect compensation but they decided to award £600 for time and trouble. If the panel recommended £1,000 compensation and we thought £100 we would not object to it, as they are the people to decide. In another complaint we thought £500 and the panel awarded £650 and the complainant turned around to me and said off the record that they did not think that was enough and they took it further to the Ombudsman and they said the offer made was more than generous.

This particular authority did not appear to mind that panels were making awards in excess of the amount that was considered 'appropriate'. However, it seems doubtful that other authorities would be as sanguine! In light of the fact that this is public money that is being spent, the preferable solution would be to have payments boards or to pass on to insurers, who should build up a consistent approach to awards. Panels have different personnel on them and are faced with one-off decisions. They are therefore liable to come to possibly very widely varying decisions, leading to inequalities in approach.

4. One complaints manager in the research came up with a novel suggestion for a panel remedy:

   I also think that apart from the monetary bit – the direct money to the relative – what would be helpful given the very severe emotional distress these people suffered would be some kind of gesture – such as payment to a charity of their choice.

Worthy although this suggestion might be, it has to be wondered what a complainant would think of such a suggestion. It is also somewhat doubtful that the director, as the person responsible for allocating public funds, would agree to such a payment. It is not to be recommended!

5. Complaints can proceed unnecessarily to panel if an apology has allegedly been sent to the complainant, but the reality is that it is not a proper apology, as the following example shows.

A complaint was made by a father that despite knowing he was the father of a child: the authority did not ask him if he was able or willing to look after his child; it refused to give him any information about his child's whereabouts with foster carers; it did not contact him when it knew the foster carers were going to apply for a residence order; and it attempted to place the baby with other adoptive parents but did not get in touch with him. All his complaints were upheld by the investigator and there was a conciliation meeting with him following this. At this meeting an action plan was drawn up. However, the case then proceeded to panel, as in writing an apology all the department did was to apologise for any distress he might have been caused by its failure to consult him. There was no recognition of all the failings identified in the investigator's report, such as the alleged rules of confidentiality being used to deny him information about his child; breach of his Article 8 rights; and for considering placing the child with 'family' when he was the father!

The importance of this illustration is to show that when an apology is given, at whatever stage, it must be properly worded and genuine. If such an apology had been sent out as a result of a panel recommendation it seems extremely likely the complainant would have pursued his case further to the Local Government Ombudsman.

6. One local authority in the research said that there would always be a recommendation made, as the panel would recommend that the complainant be thanked for bringing the issues to its notice and for the complainant's patience. Although this may be polite and sensible in a large majority of cases, one can question whether it is always appropriate to make such a recommendation. There are cases which go to panel which essentially have no merit and which involve a persistent complainant. It may not be sensible in such cases to 'reward' the complainant with the thanks of the authority.

7. An example of a situation of where a complaints manager should not be involved is shown by the following illustration:

A complaints manager, in discussing one of the complaints in which he had been involved, commented: 'I think they (the panel) felt that it was quite difficult for them to make any clear recommendations and that it should be the Assistant Director. In actual fact it was me that made that recommendation because the way it was worded was that I wrote what they said and then I had to write out a letter for the Strategic Director and within that was me thinking well what could we do here, what was available? I went and said to the manager what I had thought of and then it was passed to the Assistant Director and she approved what had been said. I was a bit worried that if they (the complainants) ever found out that those suggestions were mine and not her suggestions as to what they would do.'

The reason this was such a worrying comment is that this complaints manager had actually been personally involved in the case at an earlier stage. The complaint was on behalf of a child who had had thirteen placements in two years of local authority care.

The complaints manager had actually been in charge of the child services team towards the end of that period. So it could certainly be argued that the complaints manager was handling, reviewing and making recommendations on his own actions.

Generally speaking there is nothing wrong with a panel seeking clarification or advice from a complaints manager, but obviously it needs to be borne in mind that the panel must be the people who ultimately make a recommendation and it must not be the complaints manager.

End notes

1. SSI 1991/894.
2. *Guidance and Regulations Vol. 3* HMSO 1991.
3. SI 1738, reg. 20(2).
4. At 3.17.1. The adult procedure provides relatively clear advice as it states that both 'the clerk and the complaints manager should normally attend to provide administrative support, except where this may create a conflict of interest' but this should not unduly influence the panel's deliberations: at 3.21.1.
5. *The Right to Complain: Practice Guidance on Complaints Procedures in Social Services Departments* DoH & SSI London: HMSO 1991 at Para 4.21.
6. *Community Care Policy Guidance Annex A* para 3.
7. *Children Act Guidance* Vol. 4 Para 5.35.
8. Inspection of Complaints procedures in Local Authority Social Services Departments. Third Overview Report (1996) sss DoH, HMSO, para 4.117.
9. Ibid. para 4.118.
10. *Getting the Best from Complaints*, para 3.6.7.
11. Guidance Annex 2: Good Practice for Investigating Officers, para 3.
12. *Getting the Best from Complaints*, para 3.14.1.
13. Ibid. para 3.16.4.
14. One panel chair when interviewed, indicated that she had filing cabinets containing all of the panel papers that she had chaired over many years.
15. Some authorities have the complaints manager or other officer making the notes of the recommendations and then seeking confirmation from the chair at a later time.
16. *Community Care in the Next Decade and Beyond Policy Guidance*, HMSO, 1990, Annex A Para 7.
17. *Getting the Best from Complaints*, para 3.17.2.
18. There is a reason for the seeming tautology 'totally unanimous'. When 'a' complaint reaches panel the papers often contain a long list of complaints, some of which may have been upheld at Stage 2. At panel certainly all those complaints which have not been upheld will need consideration, as may those that have been left undecided. Even the upheld complaints may need consideration in cases where there is an issue as to the remedy the complainant is seeking. The fact that there is unanimity across all three aspects of 'a complaint' at the vast majority of panels is what is perhaps surprising.
19. One local authority taking part in the research did not realise that dissenting opinions should be recorded and only recorded the majority verdict. Thus the complainant would not have been aware of the dissenting voice.

20. This would be no different from court proceedings, where a 2:1 majority is not unusual.

21. For children, that is, although this does not have to be the case for adults: SI 2006 No 1681, para 12.

22. *The Right to Complain: Practice Guidance on Complaints Procedures in Social Services Departments* DoH & SSI London: HMSO 1991 at Para 10.25.

23. In light of this it is surprising that one Office said that they had not seen a single complaint where the panel had recommended a financial remedy or any kind of a remedy beyond an apology to the complainant and commented that this lack of remedy was why the complainants came to them.

24. NCOG Conference May 2003, *Effective complaints management: Responding to Change, Achieving Excellence.*

25. See below, under 'Other remedies'.

26. The Commission for Local Administration in England (2000) *Report on an investigation into Complaint No99/A/0761 against London Borough of Bexley* LGO: London.

27. There is a view that granting compensation or awarding sums of money might lead to resolution of the complaint and prevent the complainant from pursuing the matter further to the Local Government Ombudsman. However, there is also a risk that by making an award of money panels are acknowledging that a breach has occurred and this may give impetus to the complainant to go further. An example of such an attempt arose in Nottingham, where the local paper, *The Evening Post*, ran an article stating that a complainant was attempting to sue the local authority for £1 million. According to the press report, the complainant was basing his claim on the findings of an independent investigator's report completed at Stage 2: see the *Nottingham Evening Post* 14th November 2000

28. [2004] Q.B. 1124.

29. [2003] H.R.L.R. 4.

30. *Local Government Ombudsman Annual Report* The Stationery Office London. p 18.

31. *Remedies: Guidance on good practice*, LGO 2005.

32. See *Getting the Best from Complaints*, Chapter 6.

33. It would be of interest to know the extent to which each of these is used. However the task would be time consuming. It would require looking at one year of annual reports for 150 Authorities.

34. *Local Government Ombudsman, Annual Report 1998/99*, p11 (see also p8 of the *Annual Report 1997/1998*).

35. At 6.1.3.

36. *Complaints Procedures Directions 1990*, s.8(3), and the *Children Act Regulations*, Reg 9(1).

37. *Hadjianastassiou v. Greece* [1993] 16 EHRR 219.

38. The Commission for Local Administration in England *Report on an investigation into Complaint No. 00/C/00575 against Birmingham City Council*, York 28th September 2000 LGO: Coventry at p. 5 para 16.

39. For further discussion on the background of chairs see Chapter 3.

40. The Commission for Local Administration in England *Report on an investigation into Complaint No 99/B/3078 against Kent County Council* LGO: London

41. [1998] 2 FLR 1082.

Chapter 6

Procedure After the Panel

This chapter focuses on procedures after the panel has concluded its deliberations. The issues that will be considered are the time taken to respond to the complainant informing them of the outcome; to whom the recommendations are sent in order for the local authority to consider its final response; methods of communication between the chair and director after the panel; and whether the recommendations are followed and if this is done successfully.

Time limit for response

Regulations originally provided that the local authority had 28 days in which to decide what action to take in respect of the panel recommendations.[1] Under the new regulations this time limit has now changed and been reduced to 15 working days.[2]

Many of the authorities in the research had examples of where that did not happen and owned up to not always meeting the deadline. Particularly at certain times of the year there was a problem resulting from staff holidays, which many local authorities experienced. Particularly where this was compounded by the chair not getting the recommendations to the complaints manager as quickly as they should have been, the deadline on occasion was missed. The new deadline within which the panel recommendations need to be made[3] should mean the latter point ought to be avoided, but staff leave, especially at busy times such as Christmas, will make it very difficult to comply with the new deadline of deciding what action to take. As it is a regulation, at least in theory, it means the authority *must* respond within the deadline. However, if the time limit really cannot be met for good reason, best practice would dictate that a holding explanatory letter should be sent to the complainant. If this is done and as soon as possible thereafter the authority does respond, it is unlikely that the Local Government Ombudsman would be censorious of the authority, as the practicalities of life have to be recognised.

Where do the recommendations go?

At the time of the research social care was all contained under the one umbrella of social services. Therefore, the National Complaints Officers Group guide[4] advised that it was good practice for the director of social services to receive the panel's recommendations and make a decision on behalf of the local authority. Now the children's guidance refers to the panel recommendations going to the 'relevant director/director of Children's Services'.[5]

However, there is an issue where the director has had previous involvement with the handling of the complaint. Under normal circumstances the relevant director should not have such involvement. Unfortunately some directors, particularly those newly in post, have not realised this and have got involved in the complaint prematurely. If the director has received any complaints correspondence he should have passed it on to the complaints unit and sent a brief letter to the complainant, explaining why he could not get involved with the complaint at an early stage. If, however, this has not happened, or if, for example, the director himself was involved in some of the decision-making which the complainant is complaining about before taking up his current post, then the panel recommendations need to be sent to someone who has a similar level of authority inside the local authority.[6]

On examination of the Local Government Ombudsman reports there have been a number of instances where the director of a local authority has failed to respond at all to the complainant. For example, in a report against Kent County Council[7] it was stated that the complaints manager had promised in a letter to the complainant that the director of Kent Social Services would write having considered the panel decision. The director failed to do so and this amounted to a further example of maladministration, other than the failings already found by the panel, in the eyes of the Local Government Ombudsman [see case example 1 for a particularly bad example of where a director failed to respond to the panel recommendations and the consequent result].

Once the panel recommendations have gone to the director (or other appropriate person), the director should himself, and in the case of children in concert with the independent person appointed,[8] prepare a response to the complainant explaining whether he accepts the findings of the panel and what the authority will do in order to address any action advised.[9] The reality is that it is commonplace for the complaints manager to be the one to draft the director's response. One of the representatives of the Local Government Ombudsman commented that in some authorities the complaints manager will have a good grasp of complaints and the actions that can, and sometimes have in the past, been taken to address similar issues. The complaints manager is usually someone who is familiar with the complainant and in particular has a clear idea of what it may take to resolve the issue to the complainant's satisfaction (although in some cases it has to be acknowledged this is simply not possible). On the other hand, if the complaints manager is the one who more or less writes the response and therefore outlines the action to be taken, there may be a risk that the actions included in that response will not carry the same leverage and support when it comes to following through on the actions. Ultimately there is risk that a complaints manager will go too far in what they include in the response and further down the line they may hit a wall in terms of being able to deliver the targets identified [see case example 2 for an illustration of an especially good system]. It is therefore vital for the complaints manager to ensure, even if he does write the response, that the director gives full backing to whatever is contained in the response.

A fourth stage?

In two of the authorities covered by the research the recommendations did not pass straight on either to the director or to anyone else of a similar standing. Instead the recommendations went to a sub-committee of the council, the appeals panel, and they made a decision. Thereafter, once the complaints manager had received the minutes, a letter was drafted to the effect that cabinet had endorsed the recommendations and that went out in the director's name. That represented the final response of the local authority.

The Local Government Ombudsman was asked what its view was on such a practice and quite clearly said that it would be straightforward maladministration. There is no role for such a stage in the procedure and if the authority was introducing a Council veto then that is incorrect. In the *Beeson* case[10] a highlighted concern was the involvement of councillors in the panel proceedings and decision-making. Ultimately it was felt that the involvement of councillors at panel did not infringe the fairness of the procedure. However, there is nothing in either *Beeson*, or the previous guidance, which indicates that the practice described here is acceptable. There is a clear difference between asking two councillors to sit with an independent person and asking a whole body of councillors to consider recommendations. If the courts have some concerns about individual councillors sitting on the panel, then it would be expected that there would be great concern about introducing a fourth stage, where the decision is in the hands of a whole committee of councillors. There was therefore nothing in the past to support such a process and there is nothing in the new regulations or guidance that would permit such a procedure.

Communication between the chair and the director

The National Complaints Officers Group[11] comment that it is acceptable for the director, on receipt of the panel recommendations, to discuss the matter over the phone with the chair where the director intends to accept the recommendations, but that in circumstances where the director disputes them, the parties would need a more detailed discussion. This obviously implies that the two should meet. There is nothing in the new guidance which positively stipulates that the parties must meet. However, the guidance for both procedures, when discussing the role of the chair,[12] does state that the chair should 'be available to meet local authority staff, if needed, after the panel meeting to discuss any recommendations arising'.

Only about a quarter of the areas surveyed in the research said there was communication, either in person or on the telephone, on a regular basis between the director and the chair. This communication normally occurred when the director was seeking further clarification of the panel findings, as well as when he was in at least slight disagreement with the panel. The process was described as enabling the director to dig out and obtain any more information that he felt was required and then to let the chair and complaints manager know what he intended doing.

All the local authority areas that did have meetings between the chair and director appeared to do so very much on an individual basis, when circumstances required. Some also saw it as part of the feedback loop, particularly when using a regular chair of panels, and also so that the chair could make sure that the recommendations were followed both in spirit and to the letter. Furthermore, the view was that there can be value, where the panel have more general concerns, in expressing those concerns to the director, but not necessarily in the findings and recommendations shared with the complainant. Thus, for example, if the panel came across examples of what was suspected to be very poor practice, but which had not been explicitly complained about or explored, the chair might wish to take the opportunity to follow this up.

Not one of the complaints managers interviewed mentioned that the independent person appointed at Stage 2 regularly met with the director, despite the fact that under the previous regulations the local authority were required 'together with the independent person appointed to the panel under regulation 8(3) [to] consider what action if any should be taken in relation to the child in the light of the representation, and that independent person shall take part in any decisions about any such action'.[13] As mentioned above, the new regulations also require the independent person to be involved in the decision-making. However, neither of these regulations seems at all necessary. The independent person's role is largely to check that the investigation is carried out thoroughly and fairly and to make comments should he be in disagreement with any of the investigating officer's findings. It is the panel's job to make the ultimate findings and recommendations and it is their report which the director must consider and act upon. The independent person is not privy to the panel's discussions leading up to their report. There does not therefore seem to be any good reason for the independent person to be involved at the final decision-making stage.

Does the director follow the recommendations?

In *R v. Avon County Council, ex parte M*[14] Henry J made it clear that local authorities should normally adhere to panel findings and recommendations. He said:

> *I would be reluctant to hold (and do not) that in no circumstances whatsoever could the social services committee have overruled the review panel's recommendation in the exercise of their legal right and duty to consider it. Caution normally requires the court not to say 'never' in any* obiter dictum *pronouncement. But I have no hesitation in finding that they could not overrule that decision without a substantial reason and without having given that recommendation the weight it required.*[15]

Also, in *R v. London Borough of Brent, ex parte Sawyers*[16] the Court of Appeal noted 'it would be an unusual case when a local authority acted against the panel's recommendations.'

However, in *Listening to People* the Department of Health Advisory Group expressed concern about the failure to implement panel recommendations.[17] Paragraph 10.1 stated:

> *Confidence in the effectiveness of the procedures has also been eroded by the failure of some authorities to implement the decision made at the second stage or by review panels.*

This concern has also been expressed by the Local Government Ombudsmen in their annual reports. In a complaint against Leeds[18] it was commented that: '[The authority] failed to address the criticism made and identify action to be taken' and 'because some of the panel's criticisms did not result in specific recommendations they remained unaddressed.'

The majority finding in the research was that the director would indeed normally follow the panel's recommendations, but that occasionally the panel did not get things quite right. So, for example, the panel might make a recommendation which, in the view of the director, was too big and too general and would entail making sweeping changes on the basis of only one fairly small piece of evidence. Thus it simply would not be appropriate to agree to that recommendation.

The Local Government Ombudsman representatives were of the view that they would want to know what had happened since the recommendations were made, when considering the director's role in responding. They would expect extremely clear reasoning for not going along with what the panel had said. However, if the authority said that they could not do exactly as recommended, but were instead doing something else deemed more appropriate and set out its reasons for this, the reasons being clear and well explained, then that might well be acceptable.

Ultimately, it is clear that a director who goes against a panel's recommendations must have strong reasons for doing so.[19] Equally he must not change the recommendations without strong reasons for so doing.

Chair informed of the outcome?

Good practice dictates that it should be routine to inform the chair of the panel of the outcome of the panel in terms of the director's final response and the actions to be taken. However, for the most part the research revealed, in interviews with chairs, that chairs will normally only be informed of the details of actions taken to resolve a complaint where they pursue matters for themselves.

One chair considered it should be taken one step further and said not only did chairs need to know of the director's response, but also what had in fact been done in order to rectify the situation or prevent it from happening again. This view has some backing when considering further the Local Government Ombudsman Report involving Leeds, where the panel, too, were at fault.[20] As noted above, the Local Government Ombudsman found that the response received from the director following the panel was inadequate due to the failure to address the criticism made and to identify action to be taken. Also, neither the panel nor the director offered any remedy to the complainants for the time and trouble they had taken in pursuing the complaint, nor for the injustice suffered as a result of those parts of the complaint that had been upheld by the panel. Furthermore, in the same report, the Local Government Ombudsman identified the fact that it had taken the local authority from receipt of the panel's report in October 1999 to April 2000 to set out a clear response to each of the recommendations made by the panel and, because some of the panel's criticisms did not result in specific recommendations, they remained unaddressed even at that late stage. As a result of the report the local authority had to pay a sum of £500 to the complainants for the time and trouble involved in the complainants making the complaint and the additional stress that was caused by failing to act.

The view of the chair, who felt she should be told what had happened, was in contrast to the view of a complaints manager, who said he would be very surprised if chairs were informed, because as far as the panel were concerned they had done their bit once the findings and recommendations had been agreed by the director. Of the two points of view, there is clearly a strong argument for incorporating a report back to the panel chair into the follow up mechanism. If chairs are being appointed for their expertise and to lead on making a decision, the argument that they are one of the principal people to be notified of the decision and what steps should be taken to make that happen are fairly compelling. If chairs are not included in the follow-up mechanism there is a danger that the spirit of the recommendation may not be followed in practice and chairs may then, in time, come to experience a new complaint along exactly the same lines as previously. [However, see case example 3 for caution in expecting too much of chairs.] This could be avoided if their previous advice and recommendations has been acted upon. Further support for this view can be taken from a report against Hounslow.[21] The Local Government Ombudsman found that the director did not tell the chair of the panel what their response was to the panel's findings and recommendations until March 2000 when the panel had taken place in December 1999. This was one of a number of faults which were found to amount to repeated maladministration and as a consequence led to injustice.

Follow up of recommendations

In the research it was found that many local authorities struggled significantly in endeavouring to ensure that the recommendations arising from panel and the director's response are monitored. Some had a computer tracking package, but only a handful had used it. Clearly the follow-up system is likely to be reliant on the complaints manager to a great degree, but it is concerning if only a handful of authorities have any detailed picture of how the actions drawn up have actually been carried out, if at all. This is certainly the view of the Department of Health, in *Listening to People*.[22] It is bordering on the pointless if a complainant progresses through the lengthy complaints procedure but then the learning from the complaint remains simply in the smaller unit of the complaints section. Where this happens both the service and service users are losing out. Furthermore, it obviously potentially means that the same complaint can come through the system more than once and that in turn costs the local authority both in time and money to investigate and put right, when it is something which could easily have been avoided.

The comment by the complaints manager in one of the few authorities which excelled when it came to feedback and learning from complaints is worth repeating in full:

> When the director is making the recommendations he is also ensuring that the responsible officers are identified and aware of their responsibilities. He will say to them, 'this is what I am recommending' and that recommendation will be shared by internal memo stating what has been agreed and showing an action plan. So I get a copy of that and I will follow up at intervals to see what has happened. There have been occasions, of course, where action plans have not been put into practise on time and so I will chase them for progress and evidence of that progress just to make sure that it happens. The system we use is a *Customer Relations Management System*, which will accommodate the statutory complaints as well as our corporate procedure. Currently we use an internal database system, which has all the client records, and it has a separate *Representations module*. In its development the IT programme missed out the quality field in terms of corrective actions but we have an informal system, which is mainly paper-based. But I have just led a task group to produce specific provisions for the new system and hopefully the result will be a better system.

This authority demonstrates how much responsibility can be laid at the door of a complaints manager, but that with forward planning the problems of follow-up can be addressed. This same manager also suggested that there perhaps ought to be regular press and media releases around what has been learnt from representations and what the department were doing. That way it is demonstrated that the procedure is about both transparency and raising confidence [see case example 4 for an example of a good follow up action plan].

The view of the Local Government Ombudsman was that it would be helpful if there was further legislation or guidance on recommendations, as then their office might see council's setting up something specific to deal with the recommendations. However, the new guidance simply requires the authority to notify the complainant of his right to proceed to the Local Government Ombudsman if still dissatisfied.[23]

Certainly the Local Government Ombudsman has taken the view that where panel recommendations have not been properly implemented after an undertaking to do so, *prima facie* this would amount to maladministration.[24] In an interesting report issued against Sheffield City Council,[25] which is detailed fully here in order to demonstrate the manifold failings of the complaints system on this occasion, the Local Government Ombudsman awarded compensation after there was failure to act upon a panel's recommendation. In the particular case, the service user had learning difficulties and an autistic spectrum disorder. The service user's brother felt that his brother had not been properly assessed and supported. The Local Government Ombudsman found that there had been maladministration causing injustice. Her investigation revealed that the Council had undertaken no proper assessment when it first received a referral in 1999, kept no proper records and failed to undertake any effective service planning. The failure was compounded further after the review panel recommended that the assessment was done. A care plan had been drawn up after an assessment was completed in June 2000, but the Council's attempts to help the brothers were not successful, primarily because social services staff did not take the time to build up a relationship with the service user and as a result he had repeatedly refused services offered because he found new people and social situations frightening. His brother had requested a carer's assessment in August 2000 but the Ombudsman found no evidence that this was undertaken until November 2002. The local authority argued that it was not culpable, because the service user had rejected services when offered them. The Ombudsman accepted that services could not be forced on an unwilling person, but criticised the local authority for taking these rejections at face value rather than considering whether, given his degree of learning difficulty and autistic spectrum disorder, decisions to reject services were informed decisions. The panel had recommended that a reassessment of the needs of the complainant and his brother, as carer, should be carried out and that the Council should consider whether an apology should be made and compensation paid to the complainant. The review panel stated that its reasons for the recommendation were that:

> *Although some needs identified in the care plan were met, some were not met or monitored adequately, there was no evidence of a review being made and there had been no assessment of the needs of the complainant's brother, as a carer.*[26]

The Council responded to the review panel recommendations in July 2002. It agreed to carry out a reassessment of the service user's needs and a consideration of 'whether your brother is eligible for assessment in his own right as a carer'. It declined to pay any compensation as it did not find that 'Social Services have acted outside of Council policy or procedure'. It apologised for the 'lack of a review for the two years since the assessment and individual plan were completed in June 2000'.[27]

According to the Local Government Ombudsman the Council's handling of the case revealed a failure to take consistent action within the framework of the relevant legislation and extensive delays at many stages. These failures constituted maladministration. The Ombudsman made several recommendations, including that the local authority should comply with statutory timescales for determination of complaints under the social services statutory complaints procedure and awarded the complainant significant compensation.

In their response to the Department of Health consultation *Learning from Complaints*[28] 20 of the respondents, including 17 complaints managers, thought that the complaints manager could not ensure that recommendations are implemented but that their role is to monitor the implementation.[29] It is obvious that it is a significant failure to have a lack of systematic follow-up of recommendations. The aim of any complaints procedure should be based upon learning from both positive and poor aspects of policy and practice. Ultimately there needs to be demonstrable improvements after a justifiable complaint has been investigated in order to allow for corrective actions and learning. Whilst it is recognised that the complaints manager's role is an arduous one, it would seem that he is the obvious person to make sure that complaints recommendations are acted upon. Also, in order to achieve the best feedback and learning from complaints, there needs to be recognition, in the wider domain of the local authority, of the role that complaints can play in improving the service so that both provider and user benefit. This can be achieved by producing newsletters and circulars to be shared throughout the various departments inside the local authority. This should encourage the demystification of complaints and the value that they can inject into service provision and, at the same time, demonstrate that providers have nothing to fear from a complaints process.

Feedback from complainants about their experience of the panel

Theoretically it should not matter whether or not someone's complaint has been upheld for them to be able to comment on the actual process of the panel, but realistically most people's views are likely to be tainted by the outcome of the hearing. If all or most of their complaints have been upheld, they are much more likely to have a positive view of the procedure than if their complaints have largely or totally been rejected. Seeking feedback, therefore, has obvious difficulties.

Due to these manifest difficulties, many authorities in the research had made little or no effort to obtain their complainants views about the process. However, some of them had made various attempts and one complaints manager in particular argued that immediately after the panel has taken place is an excellent time at which to seek views, as at that time the complainant is not clouded by the actual recommendations which have been made and is merely speaking about their experience of the panel as part of the process. Other managers said that they are usually quite well aware of what the complainant thinks about the complaints system and formal feedback is a waste of time.

Concerns which had been highlighted by those local authorities which did seek feedback mainly included the surroundings where the panel was held, and, interestingly, complainants being split between either criticising the panel members for allegedly being too close to the local authority, or complaining that they felt that the people sitting on the panel should not be so independent of the authority but should be from positions within the

Local Area and have a closer understanding of how social services operate. It appears you cannot win!

Key points summary

- The authority has 15 working days in which to respond to the panel findings and recommendations.

- The panel papers should normally be sent to the director, who must not have had any previous involvement in the complaint.

- It is not permissible for another stage to be introduced into the complaints process between the panel and the director. No-one other than the director, or his representative, can take the decision after the panel.

- The director and chair should meet where the director is unsure or disagrees with the panel findings and recommendations.

- The director should normally adhere to the panel's findings and recommendations and should only depart from them when he has strong reasons for doing so.

- Despite the regulations requiring that the independent person be involved in considering what action should be taken by the director, there seems little point in this requirement.

- The chair should be informed of the outcome of the director's decision.

- A system of follow-up monitoring of the outcome should be implemented in order to ensure both that all relevant actions are indeed undertaken and that learning from the complaint occurs.

- If an authority wishes to gain feedback on the complaints process from complainants, the sensible time at which to attempt this is immediately after the panel, before its outcome is known.

Practice illustrations and case examples

1. The following illustration of a case going badly wrong is lengthy. However, it demonstrates real weaknesses when the system goes wrong and contains a number of learning points. It is therefore included in detail:

   The case was a very sad one involving adopted twin girls. They had been adopted when quite small, but sadly their early life experiences had had deep rooted effects and they had grown up to be extremely troubled and troublesome teenagers. The complaint surrounded the services being offered to the complainants and also the handling of an alleged incident of abuse of one of the girls by her father. The investigation into the complaint was complicated and hampered by the investigator's lack of access to the girls' files.

   The investigator upheld or partially upheld 8 out of 19 complaints and at the panel the findings were further altered, with more complaints being upheld. Initially there was a delay of 18 days in the chair meeting the director. However, the delay was an acceptable one, as it was due to his annual leave. When the parties did meet, the director accepted all of the findings and recommendations with one caveat. One of the recommendations was that the department should give consideration to making a financial payment to the complainants as a goodwill gesture for the failings identified in the complaint. The director, understandably, wanted to seek legal advice on this recommendation. There was also an outstanding issue concerning access to files which needed resolving. Although this was not the subject of dispute, it did just need checking. Therefore, at that stage, as far as the process was concerned, everything had gone much as it should. However, subsequently things went badly wrong.

Due to the nature of the issues involved and the remedies sought, the case needed to be dealt with swiftly and the complainants needed to know the department's response urgently. However, despite the chair telephoning the complaints manager on a number of occasions and the manager raising the case frequently with the director, over a month later still no final letter had been sent to the complainants by the director. At this point the chair wrote to him making it clear that she was extremely unhappy and the matter must be resolved with a degree of urgency.

The important point that this illustrates is that if the chair and director do not conclude matters at their meeting, the chair needs to be kept informed of what is happening and, if necessary, be active in pursuing any unfinished business.

By this time the chair had also become aware that the departmental representative at panel was wishing to challenge at least one of the findings of the panel, in view of the fact that he said there was further information in the files which had not been discussed at panel and which might alter views.

The issue here, as the chair pointed out in her letter to the director, is that this was completely unacceptable. The department cannot turn up after panel with so-called new information, but which is actually information that was available at the time of the panel. It is up to the representative to be properly prepared for panel and the department has to bear the consequences if he is not.

In response to the chair's letter the director arranged to meet her again one week later. A meeting did take place, but unfortunately the director was called away at the last minute, so an assistant director met her in his stead. This meeting went badly wrong. When the chair got there she discovered that the departmental representative had sent in a long document in response to the panel findings, challenging many of them, despite the fact that many of the faults had already been admitted at panel. The assistant director started the meeting with going through this document and defending the actions of the staff.

The action by the assistant director was not appropriate. The chair had already met the director and he had largely agreed the panel findings and recommendations. However, the assistant director seemed to want to revisit various matters to which the director had already agreed. Thus the chair had gone expecting to finalise any outstanding issues, but instead got drawn into a re-discussion. The lesson from this is that a chair needs to be firm and should not to allow a meeting to be hijacked to suit the agenda of a departmental representative. The final decision-making is up to the panel and the director, no-one else.

> *By the end of the meeting the chair had agreed that due to some information being available on one complaint, information which had not been available either to the investigator or at panel, she would check with her fellow members and ask if they would agree to slightly amend the wording of one finding. Also, as the departmental representative had provided information with confusing and contradictory dates, the complaints manager would check the accuracy of these dates. Once these two minor items had been dealt with, a letter would be sent out to the complainants. But nothing then happened. One month later still no letter had been sent to the complainants and the chair had to write to the director yet again. This was after she had badgered the complaints manager on a number of occasions and had also spoken to the assistant director. So by the time the letter was written it was three months since the panel and still the complainants had received no final response.*
>
> *The director at last sent out a final response some 11 days after this, but not surprisingly this was in effect too late and the complainants had proceeded to contact the Ombudsman. In the meantime two members of the department went out to see the complainants to discuss the panel and the response. The chair then received an e-mail from the assistant director advising her of this and included in the e-mail was the comment: 'Incidentally, I am told that Mr & Mrs X were very hostile and abusive.'*

The action by the assistant director was extraordinary and very unprofessional. It is hardly surprising, given the circumstances, that the complainants were aggressive. But, even if they were not justified in so being, this information should not have been sent to the panel chair. Their complaints had been upheld. As far as a chair is concerned that is the relevant issue.

> *Ultimately the authority did reach a local settlement with Mr and Mrs X. However, it cost the authority dear. They had to make a payment on the initial panel recommendations and a further payment for the maladministration found by the Ombudsman. The Ombudsman also recommended that the director meet with the chair and the other two panel members to discuss the case and the lessons to be learned from it, which added yet further to the expense of the whole procedure.*

This case demonstrates what can happen if a local authority lose their grip on the complaints procedure. The complainants had a very serious case to answer from the outset. Yet time and time again when the department could have retrieved the situation they missed the opportunity. This case fell far short of best practice standards.

2. One complaints manager in the research described an excellent system which was operating in his authority. The authority had a very active director, who received the papers a week in advance of a panel and always read them. At the same time an appointment was made in his diary to discuss the panel the half day after the hearing. The complaints manager would talk through anything arising and the director would

ring the chair in his presence. He had usually started to think about the response as he would have read the recommendations and he would talk that through with the complaints manager and tell the chair. He always wrote his own response letter.

Whilst quite such a Rolls Royce service is unlikely to occur in many other authorities, the basic principle of forewarning the director and perhaps booking in advance a potential telephone call/meeting with the chair, particularly where the papers indicate it is likely the panel are going to be dealing with serious matters, is a practice other authoritiess could develop to suit their own particular circumstances.

3. Although it makes sense to keep the chair informed as to the outcome of the panel, this also has to be tempered with the reality that the chair does not work for the authority and is not ultimately responsible for what happens. This point was explained by one chair in the research:

> *I think you need to see evidence of it other than just being told that it has happened. The recommendation might not have been followed up in the way that you intended. There is a weakness there, but it should not be the job of the chair to have a checklist to follow up. I would not know whom to contact and of course I have another job to be doing. I do think it is a potential weakness that the chair does not get all of the information they should. Sometimes things are so far back you forget and I am not convinced that I am always informed even where I stated that I wanted to know the outcome.'*

This demonstrates how important it is that the directors and/or complaints manager keep a firm grip on panel recommendations. Chairs are liable to become disillusioned if they consider that all the work they are putting into complaints is not being properly considered and implemented.

4. The following is an example of a good sample action plan:

Mr X: Complaints Review Panel Recommendations – Action Plan
Date of Panel: dd/mm/yy
DCO: *Mr AB*
Monitoring: *Complaints Unit*

Recommendation	Action required	Timescale Start date	Manager with responsibility
1 *Therefore the panel recommends that the director of social services asks the line manager for the complaints unit to investigate why there was such a delay progressing through this investigation. The investigation should determine whether further action needs to be taken.*	*The line manager of the complaints unit to carry out an investigation and discuss the outcome with the director.*	*21 days.*	*Mr CD*

2 *It is recommended that the director makes it absolutely clear that when the investigator's report is sent to the adjudicating officer for checking factual accuracy, that this is not used as an opportunity to challenge the investigator's conclusion.*	*The director will write to all DCOs clarifying his expectation.*	*30 days*	*director*
3 *It is recommended that the department provides Mr X with a written apology for failures identified by the complaints investigator and the review panel. The letter of apology should acknowledge the lack of:* ● *Item 1* ● *Item 2* ● *Item 3* ● *Item 4*	*Letter of apology from the director to be sent to Mr X.*	*30 days*	*director, with assistance from the complaints manager*
4 *The panel recommends that the department review the implementation of the policy and provide feedback to members. The panel recommends that this review should be completed by dd/mm/yy.*	*The director to meet with elected members to discuss this recommenda-tion.*	*By dd/mm/ yy*	*director.*

This action plan has been agreed following the director's acceptance of the panel's recommendations. All tasks are to be completed within the stated timescale. Failure to do this might result in:

(1) Ombudsman investigation
(2) complainant taking further legal action

The named manager will retain responsibility for the implementation of the recommendation until completed. If there are delays for any reason, the complainants and Complaints Unit must be notified before the timescale expires.

The action plan should be signed by the panel chair and departmental representative.

Signed: _____   Signed: _____

Panel chair   Departmental representative

The action plan includes examples of varying types of actions that might need to be taken, both by the department and by the complaints unit, with time limits. Such a plan could be easily adapted to fit the requirements of any authority.

End notes

1. Direction 8 (4) and the *Children Act* regulation 9 (3) requires that the authority shall, within 28 days, together with the IP appointed to the panel consider what action if any should be taken.
2. SI 1681, reg. 14.
3. See Chapter 5. The time limit is five working days.
4. National Complaints Officers Group (1998) *Complaints Review Panels – A Good Practice Guide* Stoke: Hamilton Training Service.
5. *Getting the Best from Complaints*, para 3.18.1. The new adult Guidance refers to the panel recommendations going to the 'relevant director': *Learning from Complaints*, para 3.23.
6. Throughout this chapter reference will simply be made to the 'director' when speaking of the responding officer in the local authority.
7. The Commission for Local Administration in England *Report on an Investigation into Complaint No 99/B/3078 against Kent County Council* 6th March 2001 LGO: Coventry at para 106.
8. But on this, see further below.
9. SI 1738, reg. 20(3) and *Getting the Best from Complaints*, para 3.18.1.
10. *R (Beeson) v. Dorset County Council & Secretary of State for Health* [2001] EWHC Admin 986, discussed in Chapter 2.
11. National Complaints Officers Group (1998) *Complaints Review Panels – A Good Practice Guide* Stoke: Hamilton Training Service.
12. See *Getting the Best from Complaints and Learning from Complaints*, Appendix 1.
13. SI 1991 No. 894 *Representations Procedure (Children) Regulations 1991*, reg 9(3).
14. [1994] 2 FLR 1006.
15. At 1019.
16. [1994] 1 FLR 203, at p.204.
17. DoH (2000) *Listening to People: A Consultation on Improving Social Services Complaints Procedures*. London: DoH.
18. The Commission for Local Administration in England *Report on an Investigation into Complaint No 00/C/04462 against Leeds City Council* 25th September 2001 LGO: York.
19. If the director wrongly fails to follow the panel's recommendations and the matter ends up in court the case of *Re S (Eligible Child)* [2008] EWCA Civ 1140 serves as warning of the court's powers. In this case a child had severe disabilities. When she was 17, her parents issued proceedings in an attempt to force the local authority to perform their statutory duty to carry out an assessment of her needs and to prepare a pathway plan for her. The local authority failed to comply with a number of court orders, so that ultimately Lord Justice Ward, in the Court of Appeal, had this to say: 'To make matters abundantly plain, and to demonstrate to the local authority that this is an order which we expect to be obeyed, this order will be endorsed with a penal notice and the director is to be given the assurance by those who represent him today that his contemptuous disregard of this order could lead to an application to commit him and, without prejudging that matter, my preliminary view is that it stands a good prospect of success and he should be advised accordingly.' At para 9.

20. The Commission for Local Administration in England *Report on an Investigation into Complaint No 00/C/04462 against Leeds City Council* 25th September 2001 LGO: York.

21. The Commission for Local Administration in England *Report on an Investigation into Complaint No 99/A/5207 against London Borough of Hounslow* 29th March 2001 LGO: London at p. 28.

22. DoH (2000) *Listening to People: A consultation on improving Social Services Complaints Procedures*. London: DoH.

23. SI 1738, reg. 20(3) and *Getting the Best from Complaints*, para 3.18.2.

24. Expressed in letters dated 2 June 1998 and 18 May 1999 to Complaints Officers Groups.

25. The Commission for Local Administration in England *Report on an Investigation into Complaint No 02/C/08690 against Sheffield City Council* 9th August 2004 LGO: York.

26. Ibid at para 34.

27. Ibid at para 35.

28. DoH *Learning From Complaints, Summary of Responses to the Consultation on Changes to the Social Services Complaints Procedure for Adults – Results of Public Consultation* January 2006.

29. Ibid. Para 3.9.2.

References

Legislation

Adoption and Child Act 2002

Children Act 1989 Representations Procedure (England) Regulations (The) 2006 (SI 17238)

Children Act Regulations Guidance and Regulations Vol.3 HMSO 1991

Children and Young Persons Representations Procedure (Children) Regulations (The) 1991 (SI 894)

Children Leaving Care Act 2000

Compensation Act 2006

Data Protection Act 1998

European Convention on Human Rights 1950

Health and Social Care act 2003

Human Rights Act 1998

Local Authority Social Services Act 1970 c.42

Local Authority Social Services and National Health Service Complaints (England) Regulations (The), 2009 DoH (SI 309)

Local Authority Social Services Complaints (England) Regulations (The) 2006 (SI 1681)

Local Government Act 2000

National Assistance Act 1948

NHS and Commununty Care Act 1990

Cases

Anurfrijeva and Another v. London Borough of Southwark [2004] QB 1124

Bernard v. LB Enfield [2003] HRLR 4

Claire F v. Secretary of State for the Home Department [2004] 2 FLR 517

Hadjianastassiou v. Greece [1993] 16 EHRR 219

McKenzie v. McKenzie [1970] 3 All ER 1034

R v. Avon County Council, ex parte M [1994] 2 FLR 1006

R v. Birmingham City Council, ex parte A [1997] 2 FCR 357

R v. Cornwall County Council, ex parte H [2000] 1 FLR 236

R v. East Sussex County Council, ex parte W [1998] 2 FLR 1082

R v. Leicester City Justices, ex parte Barrow [1991] 2 QB 260

R v. London Borough of Brent, ex parte Sawyers [1994] 1 FLR 203

R v. London Borough of Lambeth, ex parte Al-Azawi [1998] 11th June, Unreported

R v. London Borough of Sutton, ex parte Tucker [1996] 40 BMLR 137

R v. Secretary of State for the Home Department, ex parte Swati [1986] 1 WLR 477

R (Beeson) v. Dorset County Council & Secretary of State for Health [2001] EWHC Admin 986

R (on the application of Beeson) v. Secretary of State for Health [2002] EWCA Civ 1812

R (on the application of JL and another) v. Islington London Borough Council [2009] EWHC 458 (Admin)

R (on the application of LP) v. Barnet London Borough Council [2000] WL 1791622

Re S (Eligible Child) [2008] EWCA Civ 1140

Publications

Caring for People: Community Care in the Next Decade and Beyond. (1989) White Paper.

Community Care Policy Guidance. (1991) London: HMSO.

Complaints Procedures: Community Care in the Next Decade and Beyond. (1990) Policy Guidance Cm 849, London: HMSO.

Complaints Procedures Directions. (1990) London: HMSO.

Complaints Review Panels: A Good Practice Guide. (1998) National Complaints Officers Group, Hamilton Training Service, Stoke on Trent.

Get it Sorted: Providing Effective Advocacy Services for Children and Young People Making a Complaint under the Children Act 1989. (2004) DfES.

Getting the Best from Complaints: Social Care Complaints and Representations for Children, Young People and Others (2006) London: DCSF.

http://www.dcsf.gov.uk/everychildmatters/resources-and-practice/IG00152/ (correct as of January 2010).

Inspection of Complaints Procedures in Local Authority Social Services Departments (The) (1993) SSI DOH HMSO.

Inspection of Complaints Procedures in Local Authority Social Services Departments: Third Overview Report (The) (1996) SSI DOH HMSO.

Inquiry into Police Investigation of Complaints of Child and Sexual Abuse in Leicestershire Children's Homes (The) (1993) Police Complaints Authority.

Learning from Complaints (2006) DoH

http://www.dh.gov.uk/en/Consultations/Closedconsultations/DH_4102052 (correct as of January 2010).

Learning From Complaints, Summary of Responses to the Consultation on Changes to the Social Services Complaints Procedure for Adults: Results of Public Consultation (2006) DoH.

Leicestershire Inquiry 1992 (The) (1993) Andrew Kirkwood QC.

Listening to People: A Consultation on Improving Social Services Complaints Procedures (2000) London: DoH.

Pindown Experience and the Protection of Children: The Report of the Staffordshire Child Care Inquiry 1990 (The) (1991) Levy, A. and Khan, B. Staffordshire County Council.

The Right to Complain: Practice Guidance on Complaints Procedures in Social Services Departments (1991) DoH and SSI, London: HMSO.

Local Government Ombudsman Reports

The Commission for Local Administration in England *Report on an Investigation into Complaint No 05/C/06420 Against Sheffield City Council, 2006/7* Coventry: LGO: Coventry.

The Commission for Local Administration in England *Report on an Investigation into Complaint No 02/C/08690 Against Sheffield City Council 9th August 2004* LGO: York.

The Commission for Local Administration in England *Report on an Investigation into Complaint No 01/B/17272 Against London Borough of Bromley 31st July 2003* LGO: Coventry.

The Commission for Local Administration in England *Report on an Investigation into Complaint No 01/C/09018 Against Wolverhampton City Council 30th September 2002* LGO: Coventry.

The Commission for Local Administration in England *Report on an Investigation into Complaint No 01/C/07439 Against Sheffield City Council' 20th June 2002* LGO: York.

The Commission for Local Administration in England *Report on an Investigation into Complaint No 99/C/05229* Against Shropshire Council 24th January 2002 LGO: York.

The Commission for Local Administration in England *Report on an Investigation into Complaint No 00/C/04462 Against Leeds City Council 25th September 2001* LGO: York.

The Commission for Local Administration in England *Report on an Investigation into Complaint No 00/C/04462 Against Leeds City Council 25th September 2001* LGO: York.

The Commission for Local Administration in England *Report on an Investigation into Complaint No 00/C/04141 Against Lancashire County Council 30th April 2001* LGO: York.

The Commission for Local Administration in England *Report on an Investigation into Complaint No 99/A/5207 Against London Borough of Hounslow 29th March 2001* LGO: London.

The Commission for Local Administration in England *Report on an Investigation into Complaint No 99/A/00988 Against the London Borough of Southwark 12th March 2001* LGO: London.

The Commission for Local Administration in England *Report on an Investigation into Complaint No 99/B/3078 Against Kent County Council 6th March 2001* LGO: Coventry.

The Commission for Local Administration in England *Report on an Investigation into Complaint No 99/C/02624 Against Gateshead Metropolitan Borough Council 28th February 2001* LGO: York.

The Commission for Local Administration in England *Report on an Investigation into Complaint No 00/C/00575 Against Birmingham City Council, York 28th September 2000* LGO: Coventry.

The Commission for Local Administration in England *Report on an Investigation into Complaint No 99/A/0761 Against the London Borough of Bexley (2000)* LGO: London.

Local Government Ombudsman Annual Report 2003/2004. The Stationery Office: London.

Local Government Ombudsman Annual Report 1998/99. The Stationery Office: London.

Remedies: Guidance on Good Practice, LGO 2005 The Stationery Office: London.

Extracts from:
The Children Act 1989 c. 41
Part III Local Authority Support for Children and Families
Supplemental

26. Review of cases and inquiries into representations

(3) Every local authority shall establish a procedure for considering any representations (including any complaint) made to them by:

    (a) any child who is being looked after by them or who is not being looked after by them but is in need;

    (b) a parent of his;

    (c) any person who is not a parent of his but who has parental responsibility for him;

    (d) any local authority foster parent;

    (e) such other person as the authority consider has a sufficient interest in the child's welfare to warrant his representations being considered by them, about the discharge by the authority of any of their [qualifying functions] in relation to the child.

(3A) The following are qualifying functions for the purposes of subsection (3):

    (a) functions under this Part,

    (b) such functions under Part 4 or 5 as are specified by the [appropriate national authority] in regulations.

(3B) The duty under subsection (3) extends to representations (including complaints) made to the authority by:

    (a) any person mentioned in section 3(1) of the *Adoption and Children Act 2002* (persons for whose needs provision is made by the Adoption Service) and any other person to whom arrangements for the provision of adoption support services (within the meaning of that Act) extend,

    (b) such other person as the authority consider has sufficient interest in a child who is or may be adopted to warrant his representations being considered by them, about the discharge by the authority of such functions under the *Adoption and Children Act 2002* as are specified by the [appropriate national authority] in regulations.

(3C) The duty under subsection (3) extends to any representations (including complaints) which are made to the authority by:

    (a) a child with respect to whom a special guardianship order is in force,

    (b) a special guardian or a parent of such a child,

(c)   any other person the authority consider has a sufficient interest in the welfare of such a child to warrant his representations being considered by them, or

(d)   any person who has applied for an assessment under section 14F(3) or (4), about the discharge by the authority of such functions under section 14F as may be specified by the [appropriate national authority] in regulations.

(4)   The procedure shall ensure that at least one person who is not a member or officer of the authority takes part in:

(a)   the consideration; and

(b)   any discussions which are held by the authority about the action (if any) to be taken in relation to the child in the light of the consideration but this subsection is subject to subsection (5A).

(4A) Regulations may be made by the [appropriate national authority] imposing time limits on the making of representations under this section.

(5)   In carrying out any consideration of representations under this section a local authority shall comply with any regulations made by the [appropriate national authority] for the purpose of regulating the procedure to be followed.

(5A) Regulations under subsection (5) may provide that subsection (4) does not apply in relation to any consideration or discussion which takes place as part of a procedure for which provision is made by the regulations for the purpose of resolving informally the matters raised in the representations.

(6)   The [appropriate national authority] may make regulations requiring local authorities to monitor the arrangements that they have made with a view to ensuring that they comply with any regulations made for the purposes of subsection (5).

(7)   Where any representation has been considered under the procedure established by a local authority under this section, the authority shall:

(a)   have due regard to the findings of those considering the representation; and

(b)   take such steps as are reasonably practicable to notify (in writing):

(i)   the person making the representation;

(ii)   the child (if the authority consider that he has sufficient understanding); and

(iii) such other persons (if any) as appear to the authority to be likely to be affected, of the authority's decision in the matter and their reasons for taking that decision and of any action which they have taken, or propose to take.

(8)   Every local authority shall give such publicity to their procedure for considering representations under this section as they consider appropriate.

Extracts from: The Children Act 1989 Representations Procedure (England) Regulations 2006

9. Time limit on making representations

(1) A complainant must make his representations about a matter no later than one year after the grounds to make the representations arose.

(2) But a local authority may consider any representations which have been made outside the time limit specified in paragraph (1) if, having regard to all the circumstances, they conclude that:

(a) it would not be reasonable to expect the complainant to have made the representations within the time limit; and

(b) notwithstanding the time that has passed it is still possible to consider the representations effectively and fairly.

18. Request for review panel

(2) A request under paragraph (1) must be made within 20 working days of the date on which the complainant received the notice of the local authority's response and must set out the reasons for the complainant's dissatisfaction with the outcome of the investigations.

19. Review panel

(1) Where the local authority have received a request in accordance with regulation 18 they must appoint a panel to consider the representations.

(2) The panel shall consist of three independent persons, one of whom will chair the panel.

(3) The independent person appointed in accordance with regulation 17(2) may not be a member of the panel.

(4) The panel shall meet within 30 working days of the local authority receiving a request in accordance with regulation 18.

(5) At its meeting the panel shall consider:

(a) any oral or written submissions made by:

(i) the complainant or, where one has been appointed, by his advocate on his behalf;

(ii) the local authority; and

(iii) such other person as the panel consider has sufficient interest in the representations to warrant his submissions being considered by them; and

(b) any oral or written submissions which the independent person appointed in accordance with regulation 17(2) wishes to make.

(6) If the complainant attends the meeting of the panel he may be accompanied throughout the meeting by his advocate, where one has been appointed, and by another person of his choice, and may nominate the advocate or that other person to speak on his behalf.

20. Recommendations

(2) Within 5 working days of the meeting the panel must send its report to:
   (a) the local authority;
   (b) the complainant and, where one has been appointed, his advocate;
   (c) the independent person appointed under regulation 17(2); and
   (d) any other person whom the panel consider has sufficient interest in the case to warrant their receiving such a notice.

(3) Within 15 working days of receiving the panel's recommendations the local authority must, together with the independent person appointed under regulation 17(2), consider the recommendations and determine:
   (a) how the authority will respond to them; and
   (b) what they propose to do in the light of them,
   and send to the complainant its response and proposals, along with information about making a complaint to a Local Commissioner.

Appendix 3

Extracts from:
The Local Authority Social Services and National Health Service Complaints (England) Regulations 2009

3. Arrangements for the handling and consideration of complaints
(1) Each responsible body must make arrangements ("arrangements for dealing with complaints") in accordance with these Regulations for the handling and consideration of complaints.
(2) The arrangements for dealing with complaints must be such as to ensure that:
    (a) complaints are dealt with efficiently;
    (b) complaints are properly investigated;
    (c) complainants are treated with respect and courtesy;
    (d) complainants receive, so far as is reasonably practical:
        (i) assistance to enable them to understand the procedure in relation to complaints; or
        (ii) advice on where they may obtain such assistance;
    (e) complainants receive a timely and appropriate response;
    (f) complainants are told the outcome of the investigation of their complaint; and
    (g) action is taken if necessary in the light of the outcome of a complaint.

5. Persons who may make complaints
(1) A complaint may be made by:
    (a) a person who receives or has received services from a responsible body; or
    (b) a person who is affected, or likely to be affected, by the action, omission or decision of the responsible body which is the subject of the complaint.
(2) A complaint may be made by a person (in this regulation referred to as a representative) acting on behalf of a person mentioned in paragraph (1) who:
    (a) has died;
    (b) is a child;
    (c) is unable to make the complaint themselves because of:
        (i) physical incapacity; or
        (ii) lack of capacity within the meaning of the Mental Capacity Act 2005; or
    (d) has requested the representative to act on their behalf.
(3) Where a representative makes a complaint on behalf of a child, the responsible body to which the complaint is made:

(a) must not consider the complaint unless it is satisfied that there are reasonable grounds for the complaint being made by a representative instead of the child; and

(b) if it is not so satisfied, must notify the representative in writing, and state the reason for its decision.

(4) This paragraph applies where:

(a) a representative makes a complaint on behalf of:

(i) a child; or

(ii) a person who lacks capacity within the meaning of the Mental Capacity Act 2005; and

(b) the responsible body to which the complaint is made is satisfied that the representative is not conducting the complaint in the best interests of the person on whose behalf the complaint is made.

(5) Where paragraph (4) applies:

(a) the complaint must not be considered or further considered under these Regulations; and

(b) the responsible body must notify the representative in writing, and state the reason for its decision.

(6) In these Regulations any reference to a complainant includes a reference to a representative.

14. Investigation and response

(1) A responsible body to which a complaint is made must:

(a) investigate the complaint in a manner appropriate to resolve it speedily and efficiently; and

(b) during the investigation, keep the complainant informed, as far as reasonably practicable, as to the progress of the investigation.

(2) As soon as reasonably practicable after completing the investigation, the responsible body must send the complainant in writing a response, signed by the responsible person, which includes:

(a) a report which includes the following matters:

(i) an explanation of how the complaint has been considered; and

(ii) the conclusions reached in relation to the complaint, including any matters for which the complaint specifies, or the responsible body considers, that remedial action is needed; and

(b) confirmation as to whether the responsible body is satisfied that any action needed in consequence of the complaint has been taken or is proposed to be taken;

(c) where the complaint relates wholly or in part to the functions of a local authority, details of the complainant's right to take their complaint to a Local Commissioner under the Local Government Act 1974; and

(d) except where the complaint relates only to the functions of a local authority, details of the complainant's right to take their complaint to the Health Service Commissioner under the 1993 Act.

(3) In paragraph (4), ''relevant period'' means the period of 6 months commencing on the day on which the complaint was received, or such longer period as may be agreed before the expiry of that period by the complainant and the responsible body.

(4) If the responsible body does not send the complainant a response in accordance with paragraph (2) within the relevant period, the responsible body must:

(a) notify the complainant in writing accordingly and explain the reason why; and

(b) send the complainant in writing a response in accordance with paragraph (2) as soon as reasonably practicable after the relevant period.

Appendix 4

Extracts from:
Getting the Best from Complaints
Social Care Complaints and Representations for Children, Young People and Others

3.9 Stage 3 – Review Panels

3.9.1 Where Stage 2 of the complaints procedure has been concluded and the complainant is still dissatisfied, he will be eligible to request further consideration of the complaint by a Review Panel (regulation 18). As it is not possible to review a complaint that has not yet been fully considered at Stage 2 (including providing the report(s) and adjudication to the complainant), it is essential that the local authority does not unnecessarily delay the conclusion of Stage 2.

3.9.2 Further consideration of the complaint can include, in a limited number of cases, early referral to the Local Government Ombudsman (see Annex 3). Otherwise, the complainant retains the right to proceed to a Review Panel.

3.9.3 The Complaints Manager should assess requests for the Review Panel as they are presented on a case by case basis. The Complaints Manager should also confer with the Chair, following the Chair's appointment, regarding arrangements for the Panel.

3.10 Purpose of Review Panels

3.10.1 Review Panels are designed to:

- listen to all parties;
- consider the adequacy of the Stage 2 investigation;
- obtain any further information and advice that may help resolve the complaint to all parties' satisfaction;
- focus on achieving resolution for the complainant by addressing his clearly defined complaints and desired outcomes;
- reach findings on each of the complaints being reviewed;
- make recommendations that provide practical remedies and creative solutions to complex situations;
- support local solutions where the opportunity for resolution between the complainant and the local authority exists;
- to identify any consequent injustice to the complainant where complaints are upheld, and to recommend appropriate redress; and
- recommend any service improvements for action by the authority.

Complaints Panels in Social Care © Catherine Williams and Katy Ferris 2010 www.russellhouse.co.uk

3.10.2 As a general rule, the Review Panel should not reinvestigate the complaints, nor should it be able to consider any substantively new complaints that have not been first considered at Stage 2.

3.10.3 Ideally, no party should feel the need to be represented by lawyers at the Review Panel. The purpose of the Panel is to consider the complaint and wherever possible, work towards a resolution. It is not a quasi-judicial process and the presence of lawyers can work against the spirit of openness and problem-solving. However, the complainant has the right to bring a representative to speak on his behalf.

3.11 General principles

3.11.1 The Review Panel should be alert to the importance of providing a demonstrably fair and accessible process for all participants. Many complainants, particularly children and young people, may find this stage to be a stressful experience. It is important that the Panel is customer-focused in its approach to considering the complaint and child or young person-friendly. This may include limiting the total number of local authority representatives attending to a workable minimum to avoid the possibility of overwhelming the complainant.

3.11.2 In particular, the following principles should be observed for the conduct of the panel:

- The local authority should recognise the independence of the Review Panel and in particular, the authority of the Chair;

- Panels should be conducted in the presence of all the relevant parties with equity of access and representation for the complainant and local authority;

- Panels should uphold a commitment to objectivity, impartiality and fairness, and ensure that the rights of complainants and all other attendees are respected at all times;

- The local authority should consider what provisions to make for complainants, including any special communication or mobility needs or other assistance;

- Panels should observe the requirements of the Human Rights Act 1998, the Data Protection Act 1998, and other relevant rights-based legislation and conventions in the discharge of their duties and responsibilities;

- The standard of proof applied by Panels should be the civil standard of 'balance of probabilities' and not the criminal standard of 'beyond all reasonable doubt.' This standard will be based on evidence and facts; and

- It will be at the Chair's discretion to suspend or defer proceedings in exceptional circumstances where required, including the health and safety of all present.

3.11.3 The local authority should be mindful of the specific needs of children and young people either using or affected by complaints. Local authorities should ensure that:

- the Review Panel acts in accordance with the United Nations Convention on the Rights of the Child;

- the Review Panel safeguards and promotes the rights and welfare of the child or young person concerned;

- the wishes and feelings of such children and young people are ascertained, recorded and taken into account;

- the best interests of such child or young person are prioritised at all times; and

- where the complaint is made by a person deemed to have a sufficient interest in the child's welfare, they should where appropriate, seek the child or young person's views with regard to the complaint.

3.12 Redress

3.12.1 Under Section 92 of the Local Government Act 2000, local authorities are empowered to remedy any injustice arising from maladministration. Further details on remedies and redress are discussed in section 6.2.

3.12.2 The Review Panel must set out its recommendations to the local authority on any strategies that can assist in resolving the complaint. These may include financial compensation or other action within a specified framework to promote resolution.

3.13 Make up of the Panel

3.13.1 The Panel must consist of three independent people (regulation 19(2)). Independent means a person who is neither a member nor an officer of the local authority to which the representations have been made, nor the spouse or civil partner of such a person. The Independent Person appointed to Stage 2 may not be a member of the Panel (regulation 19(3)).

3.13.2 In selecting the Panel the local authority should consider:

- the profile of the local population;

- how best to demonstrate independence of the procedure;

- the needs and circumstances of the individual complainant and the need for specialist skills, knowledge, or awareness regarding the presenting complaint;

- any real or perceived conflict of interest raised by either the substance of the complaint or the Panel process for considering that complaint; and

- due care regarding political sensitivity.

3.13.3 One member of the Panel should be assigned as Chair of the panel. The Chair's role is described in Annex 1. Good practice suggests that the person appointed as Chair should not have been an officer or a Member of the local authority during the three years preceding the Panel.

3.13.4 In order that the Chair may contribute to the organisation of the panel, the Complaints Manager should appoint the Chair first – ideally within ten working days of the complainant's request to proceed to Stage 3 – before identifying other panel members.

3.14 Administration of the Panel

3.14.1 Local authorities should:

- demonstrate an ongoing commitment to supporting Panellists through regular training;

- confirm references, Criminal Records Bureau referrals, confidentiality and disclosure protocols, declarations of interest, and provide other support as required;

- provide Panellists with a letter of appointment explaining the Review Panel process, their role as a Panellist and describing the expenses and other payment to which they may be entitled. Attention should also be drawn to important issues such as confidentiality;

- reimburse Investigating Officers, Independent Persons and any other external people involved in the earlier stages for their attendance at the Panel, as appropriate;

- provide complainants with information on attending the Panel and assistance that they can draw on; and

- facilitate the administrative support and advisory functions on the day of the Panel.

3.14.2 The Panel must be held within 30 working days of the receipt of a request for a Review (regulation 19(4)). The local authority should acknowledge the complainant's request for a Review in writing within 2 days of receiving it. The Panel Review should be provided locally and with due regard to the complainant's availability and convenience. The complainant should be notified of the Panel's date and location in writing at least 10 working days before the Review Panel meets and be invited to attend.

3.14.3 Panel papers should be sent to panellists and other attendees as soon as these have been agreed by the Chair and no later than ten working days before the date of the Panel. These should normally include: information on Stage 1 (as relevant), the Stage 2 investigation report(s), the local authority's adjudication, any policy, practice or guidance information relevant to the complaint, and any comments that the complainant has submitted to the Panel. The papers should also include information on any local practice around Panels, such as conduct, roles and responsibilities.

3.14.4 If any other written material is submitted for consideration by the panel outside of these timescales, it will usually be at the Chair's discretion whether it is accepted.

3.14.5 If any complaint is logged on the day by the complainant about the proceedings, the local authority should record it and the Panel should take a view on the need for further action and should record their decision.

3.15 Attendance at the Panel

3.15.1 The complainant has a right to attend the Panel and should be assisted in attending as appropriate. The complainant should also be informed of his entitlement to be accompanied by another person and for this person to speak on his behalf.

3.15.2 Those persons involved with the investigation at Stage 2 (e.g. the Investigating Officer, and the Independent Person) should be invited to attend and contribute as relevant to their roles. Should any of these persons' unavailability cause an inordinate delay in holding the Panel; the Chair should take a view on proceeding without them. The local authority can also proceed with the Panel in the complainant's absence at the complainant's request.

3.15.3 The Adjudicating Officer should attend as the authority's representative if he has rejected any of the Investigating Officers findings at Stage 2. Where he has accepted all of them, it is usually acceptable to delegate this responsibility.

3.15.4 The Chair should make the final decision on attendees (including asking the local authority to make specific members of staff available to provide specialist advice or opinion). He should also decide whether additional policies or procedures should be circulated with the Panel's papers.

3.15.5 The Complaints Manager and anyone providing administrative support (see Annex 1) should also attend the Panel.

3.16 Conduct of the Panel

3.16.1 The Panel should be conducted as informally as possible, but in a professional manner and in an atmosphere that is accommodating to all attendees. This is particularly important where the complainant might be a child or young person. The need for other support in response to diversity and disability issues should be catered for, including (but not limited to) provision for sensory impairment, translation and interpretation.

3.16.2 Panels should normally be structured in three parts: pre-meeting, presentations and deliberations.

Pre-meeting

3.16.3 This is an opportunity for the Panellists and their administrative support to meet in closed session to discuss the order of business and any other relevant issues (e.g. taking legal advice). No deliberations on the complaint should commence at this meeting.

Presentations

3.16.4 Once all attendees are present, the Chair should commence the Review by explaining its purpose and the need for confidentiality. The Chair should advise the complainant of the respective roles and responsibilities of those present and address any questions or concerns that the complainant may have about the process.

3.16.5 The Chair should ensure that the Panel's focus is on the agreed complaint and the complainant's desired outcomes from the Stage 2 investigation. The purpose of hearing the presentations is to understand each party's opinion of the complaint rather than an opportunity to cross-examine attendees. The Chair should also indicate how long the Panellists anticipate that the presentations should last.

3.16.6 The full Panel meeting should begin with presentations on the points of complaint and desired outcomes by the complainant and the local authority. Normally, the first presentation should be by the complainant (or advocate/representative) who should be invited to 'talk' to the complaint and expand upon any relevant themes that should aid the Panel's deliberation. The Chair should ensure that this presentation is reasonable and relevant, exercising discretion in limiting its scope, substance or duration.

3.16.7 Panellists should then have sufficient opportunity to ask questions of all present and seek clarification on the issues being discussed so they are in a position to make recommendations regarding the outcome. The Chair should also invite the complainant, the local authority and other attendees to ask questions and raise points of information and opinion as relevant to the complaint.

3.17 Deliberations

3.17.1 The Panel should then go into closed session to deliberate on their findings and conclusions. The Panel may need administrative support at this stage, but this should not unduly influence the Panel's deliberations and no conflict of interest should arise.

3.17.2 The Panel is required to produce a written report containing a brief summary of the representations and their recommendations for resolution of the issues (regulation 20(1)). They must send this to the complainant, the local authority, the independent person from Stage 2 and any other person with sufficient interest within 5 working days of the Panel meeting (regulation 20(2)). The written record should set out simply and clearly a brief summary of the representations; their recommendations for the resolution of the issues and the reasons for them. If a Panellist disagrees with the majority recommendation, this should also be recorded and the reason for it given.

3.18 After the Panel

3.18.1 The local authority must send its response to the Panel's recommendations to the complainant (and other participants as necessary) within 15 days of receiving the Panel's report (regulation 20(3)). The response should be developed by the relevant Director / Director of Children's Services setting out how the local authority will respond to the recommendations and what action will be taken. If the Director deviates from the Panel's recommendations he should demonstrate his reasoning in the response. In developing his response he should invite comment from all the attendees including the Independent Person from Stage 2 (regulation 20(3)).

3.18.2 The complainant should be advised of his right to refer his complaints (if still dissatisfied) to the Local Government Ombudsman (regulation 20(3)).

3.19 Summary of stage 3 timescales

Action	Time
Complainant requests Review Panel	Up to 20 working days after receipt of the Stage 2 adjudication

Complaints Manager acknowledges request	Within 2 working days
Complaints Manager appoints Chair and confirms attendees and content of Panel papers with Chair	Within 10 working days of the complainant's request for Review Panel
Local authority agrees the other Panellists and date for Review Panel	Within 30 working days of the complainant's request for Review Panel
Local authority circulates Panel papers	Within 10 working days of the date for the Review Panel
Review Panel produces its written report (including any recommendations)	Within 5 working days of the Review Panel
Relevant Director issues his response	Within 15 working days of receiving the Review Panel's report

Quick Reference List